Dark Psychology Secrets

An Introducing Guide to Manipulation, Persuasion, NLP, Vampirism and to Learn How to Manipulate and Influence People and How to Defend Yourself through Emotional and Mind Control

Bran Deep

Table of Contents

Introduction

The human mind is perhaps the single most powerful organ in the body. It controls and directs all activities that the body does. Wise people say that taking care of the mind is like opening the gateway to great success. When it is calm, the brain helps you make decisions that lead to fruitful results. On the contrary, when the mind is weak, you make poor decisions that land you into trouble.

Psychology identifies as the study of human mind and behavior. It is a multidisciplinary concept that combines sports, social behavior, clinical, and human development aspects to achieve a wholesome description of this connection. It is an educational, theoretical, and applied science concept that offers an understanding of how the human brain functions.

Over the past few decades, the field of psychology has attracted the attention of scholars and experts as the need to enhance education, relationships, and employment, as well as the necessity of understanding basic lifestyles and treating mental conditions and illnesses.

In its purest form, psychology attempts to study people to know what and who they indeed are. It helps to appreciate the in-depth connection between the mind and the body. Through core psychological concepts, we can improve our decision-making capability and walk through stressful situations successfully. We can learn to differentiate between what's right for us and what we shouldn't tolerate in our lives. We can learn to set smart goals and enhance our livelihoods.

Furthermore, psychology not only helps you to become more successful, but it also influences your health substantially. Its contribution to the mental illness diagnosis and development of treatment cannot be understated. It has helped many people live their lives free of restrictions by mental disorders. Today there is a large number of people suffering from stress, anxiety, and depression, hence, the need for psychologist's expertise to treat this condition.

Among the various branches of psychology, there is positive psychology and dark psychology. The latter identifies as the study of the human condition of predating on others. Every person can victimize others using psychological techniques. Most people restrain this tendency of their social condition, but others leverage these impulses. While most use psychology to shed light in our lives, others continuously look for ways of using psychological techniques to fulfill selfish motives.

Dark psychology, therefore, is simply the dark side of human consciousness. It is the concept of predicting the reaction of another to a particular situation and twisting the case to obtain selfish favors. Through dark psychology, it helps us understand that predatory behaviors in society are always purpose driven. Malicious people take deliberate moves with the hope of achieving a selfish goal. It also helps us to understand that manipulators do not have any concern for other people but themselves. The concept of dark psychology can explain most criminal and deviant behaviors in society.

People with dark personality traits are found everywhere in society, including our homes, workplaces, schools, and in all our universal joints. They can spot a target and devise an excellent technique to obtain favor from them. Fortunately, we can learn to protect ourselves from the manipulation of these toxic individuals. Since dark psychology deciphers the potential for evil in all our surroundings, it is good to understand and protect yourself. You never know when you can fall victim.

Chapter 1: What Is Dark Psychology

Dark psychology is the study of a human status in its connection to the people's psychological nature to prey upon other people. The entire humanity possesses a certain potential to victimize not only their fellow human beings but also other living creatures. Whereas, other individuals who might want to sublimate or restrain this kind of tendency, there are also others who opt to act upon some of these impulses. What dark psychology seeks to achieve is to make one understand those perceptions, feelings, and thoughts that end up leading to the predatory behavior of human beings. Dark psychology assumes this type of production is done for a given purpose and contains certain goal-oriented and rational motivation nearly all the time. The remaining portion of this time is essentially the dangerous victimization of other people with no purposive intent. In other words, it can also be defined by both religious doctrine and evolutionary science.

The famous quote that knowledge is power is rarely expanded to bring out more meaning. If knowledge is power as claimed in the quote, then possessing enough knowledge of the psychology of the human can just be compared to having some superpowers. The understanding of the mind of a human being and how it operates is what is referred to as psychology. It is one of the topics that are very dear to the whole generation of human beings.

Psychology tends to underpin nearly all things from religion to crime, finance to marketing, and hate to love. Very few people have this type of privilege. It is not easy to get psychological knowledge. Just as it is with the rest of the most advanced secrets of human beings, the psychological know-how is usually covered deep within the pages of heavy journals and they are heavily guarded and kept far from the reach of the general public. To distill this kind of information into some useful forms, a person would be forced to look into several journals and books and try and separate the useless from the useful.

Having explained that, we can now get back to the topic of dark psychology. The work of dark psychology can be seen all over the world. It is a fact that many might not rejoice in it, but again, nobody can change it. With that, you are only left with this choice; you either opt to stay ignorant of a very powerful phenomenon and stand at a risk of being victimized by these mighty powers, or opt to assume full control of your situation and devise ways of safeguarding yourself, as well as the lives of the people you care for.

Comprehending the whole topic of dark psychology is not a defensive measure. There are several principles and ideas that are contained within the space of dark psychology and can greatly assist a person to improve in both their professional and personal endeavors.

Chapter 2: Fear

What's the fear?

We ideally learn from our mistakes. We also have a tendency to relive our mistakes in our minds. Things and actions that we take, which can be from everyday living and doing basic things, to the extremity of our lives being threatened, are all elements that can lead us to the feeling of fear.

Practitioners of dark psychology understand the basic form of this emotion and prey on it, whether consciously or subconsciously. They do this by inspiring and taking us to this emotion.

Fear is a very complex emotion. When we define it, we can learn what is happening to us while we are afraid. There are many physiological facets of fear, from a tingle to a scream. The way we are going to attempt to define fear is to start with the small and work to horror.

Fear is anxiety. It is the worry of something that we cannot control, possibly something that will affect us in a negative way. We process anxiety by gearing up. Our chemical makeup changes and we begin to see ourselves grind to a halt. This defensive mechanism is ancient. We perceive dangers around us and we get anxious about them.

Anxiety can also lead to a jumpiness—the cat in a room full of rocking chairs, worrying about its tail getting smashed. It shortens our fuses so that we jump at almost everything, even if that thing will not harm us.

Fear is an edginess. It is the uneasiness that we experience when we know something is about to happen. This wonderment that we can perceive something harmful before it happens touches our most basic survival instincts. We all can hunt and at the same time are hunted. The ability to feel edginess and uneasiness is a minor form of fear that can make us able to escape danger.

This edgy for of apprehension can make it so that we do not function well. It can possibly get in the way of our goals. A large part of dark psychology is another finding out what your goals are and then reminding you that you will not achieve them. This is the negativity that raises apprehension inside us, and that can be used to control.

When we dread something, it is a form of fear. The fear of doing something is always a part of us. This dread can keep us at bay. We can self-induce dread, or it can come from an outside source. Dread is the part of fear that makes us want to deflect to another topic, or makes us miserable about the grind of what we have to do.

When dread is expressed, we begin to worry. Worry is yet another form of fear. Worry is the moment we give into the thoughts or actions of dread. It is the surrender itself. When we feel like we cannot get what we need, this is not a true deterrent. Worry is the implementation of this. It is an active emotion versus a passive one.

Fear also happens when we are overwhelmed. With the practice of dark psychology, overwhelming another can be a very effective way to control them. The piling on of other things can make it so that the victim has nothing left within them to work on their original need. We do this to ourselves, by ourselves, with a thing called distraction. We are easily distracted and then we begin to create fear and wonder why we are overwhelmed.

This overwhelmed state can lead to hysteria. Hysteria is a part of fear. It is the moment where we begin to lose all control over what is actually happening in front of us. We go into a state of panic so great that we can no longer get anything done. It is a fear of the freeze. A panic of great magnitude. It is an attempt to escape the terror, that terror being life threatening or not.

Fear is a shock to our systems. It is the jolt that reminds us that we are finite and that we can lose life at any moment. Fright happens when we are overstimulated by an outside force. We get scared by things that we know are not the norm. This abnormal is where the dark play, to accomplish need quickly.

Terror is the extreme of fear. It is the amplification of all the above forms of fear. It takes us from a moment of panic to something far more severe. Creating terror in another requires very complex maneuvers. Normally it is situational. Terror takes a great toll on our systems. Since it is an extreme emotion, the process to keep it going is extreme. We do not naturally go to a state of terror, otherwise we would constantly be drained.

Placing us in a state of terror requires mastery of what makes us fear. One of the things that takes us directly there is…

Horror. Horror is something that most would consider the ultimate fear. We often recognize that things of horror cannot be unseen. They cannot be unfelt. They are not the passing fear or anxiety; they are something that strikes us straight to our core. Horror affects us and takes us to a place of hunted, or it indulges the hunter.

The mild side of horror is dismay. The horror of something not going our way is a reminder that there are no defined terms of any emotion. Dismay happens when something does not go our way. This is not necessarily the ultimate fear. However, emotions and mental study remains subjective. It is unique to the viewer and subject.

The horror that incites the most fear is the horror of gore. It is the fear that we are going to be ravaged and devoured. The horrors of war come to mind. Human men and women, animal and environment, torn apart by destructive force, and the ravages left behind. This is one of the ultimate horrors of fear. It can also be taken from a grand stage to a private stage and horror can take place in our own space. The practitioner of dark psychology can incite horror for whatever reason, or perhaps no reason at all other than it is a passing choice.

There are many things that can prompt fear in us. Some are of course, extreme. Since we are going to focus on the milder side of dark psychology, we can look at the more mundane things that cause fear in us.

Our pasts are a huge motivator of fear. When we know that something has frightened us in the past, we know it can be done again. Yes, we can indeed improve ourselves so that fear is not as extreme as it was the first time we experienced it. In this lies a truth. When we experience fear and survive, we learn. This knowledge makes it so that the next time we experience the same fear, it is not as extreme as the first time. This is a defense against dark psychology, and we will look at how to practice that in a later chapter.

The past is what goes into our minds. We are vast storage facilities for information. Those things that affect us most directly are more likely to be stored with higher priority than little tiny scares. Someone coming up and saying "boo" to you will not be remembered with the same priority than say, someone beating you.

There is a common past we all share. The fact that we are social creatures creates a social past. A community past, whether we forget or relive can be preyed upon by the dark. It is the thing we have in common that makes us connect. When the common thing that connects us is fear, that can be a strength or a weakness. Most consider communal fear to be something that will take us to a negative.

When we believe we are helpless, we give into this negative communal fear. What we choose to believe in is so crucial to how we are affected by outside forces. Some take this to an extreme and do not believe in anything, therefore creating a space of invulnerability. Most of us, however, believe in something.

What we choose to believe in can affect how much fear will influence us.

The dark practitioner uses our beliefs to touch on our fears. They will even go so far as to change our beliefs. There is a massive difference from having faith versus having an idea. The dark plays to our faiths.

Faith is more powerful than an idea. Faith is an idea with a dogma attached. This is not necessarily a religious idea. Our faith in society can be dogma. With this power comes a responsibility that has, what some consider, been taken too lightly. It is the dark that find the cracks in faith, and this is the breakdown of what we believe. They can also use this faith to gain quick advantage, knowing that we are vulnerable when we believe.

During this moment of vulnerability, injecting a little fear, can allow massive control. This is how the human fear works. We fear for our lives. We believe that there are things that can keep us safe. The dark break down those things and step in.

Given the considerable amount of ways to manipulate us with fear, there are many things that happen to us after we experience this emotion. After we experience fear we tend to be dazed and confused. This is a very vulnerable time for us. When we lose the focus of attention on what is happening, we have difficulty remaining in control. It is very easy for another to take that control from us during this time, even for a short period of time.

When we come out of fear, we feel isolated. Being the social creatures we are, being alone is not something we want to experience after we are scared. This is a powerful way to intervene into someone's life in a dark way. When we fear and then become isolated, we tend to grab onto convenience, looking for something to make us more connected.

Those who feed upon others in this state are considered vampires. It is the intention of the individual who steps in at this vulnerable moment that defines dark or light. Vampires are said to feed without remorse for both survival and enjoyment purposes.

How can we control it?

Meet your Anxiety

Sometimes, the more that we try to fight or change something just to feel good, the more it stays the same. The energy that we put into that is exhausting. In this case, try to tell yourself not to think of pink gorillas and see how it works!

Anxious thoughts take you a lot of precious mental space and even draw on our emotions, imaginations, focus, and thoughts. The more we try to control them, make sense of them, the more that they feed into our anxiety.

Try to accept being with your anxiety, without trying to change it. Accepting your anxious thoughts and feelings doesn't make them stronger or stay longer. In fact, they cease when you stop feeding them with your energy.

What you have your focus on becomes potent. So the more you focus on something, the more it grows and flourishes to expand. Therefore, try to stop yourself from pushing your anxiety away. Without forcing your anxiety to go away will bring you an understanding of it so you can deal with it.

Exercise accepting your feeling as they are for about two minutes. This is not easy, but this is powerful. Start with little bits and work up from there. If you can work on it for more than 10 minutes (sitting with your anxious thoughts like they are something natural), then the better it is for you. After a few minutes, give them your full attention and try transforming them into something else. See how it feels when you're ready and works on it longer.

Clear your Filter

Experiences from the past as well as messages have their way of changing the filter through which we view life, and the world is living. This is how it works for us regardless of the presence of anxiety in our life.

Try to see moments and experiences as though they occur for the first time in your life even when you have experienced them too many times in the past and yet, no one will be exactly like what you are facing in the present moment. Notice the difference between what is happening now and what has happened before.

Every, the time you experience it, you are changing for the better –
more brave, wise, strong, and more capable of dealing with your
anxiety though there are times when you are more anxious and more
worried.

Be open to new possibilities that come with this new experience
because that's what it is, a whole new experience!

Let's say you have a painful breakup with a long-time relationship, so
there's always this tendency to hold on back from opening your heart
to a new relationship. A new relationship with a new individual can
feel too risky for you and this is understandable.

For you, staying away and avoiding people is a move that will keep
you safe and secured. But somehow, this will take you away from
possibilities that are just there waiting for you to find them. Growth
can happen when we choose to open up ourselves to what is coming
rather than avoiding new experiences just because we are greatly
affected by what has happened in the past.

Accept Uncertainty

Anxiety can easily cause a stir because the future is always uncertain.
Not all things can go according to plan and the more we try to control
every situation, the more we should realize that we have little control
over it.

Try to let go of the need to be certain at all times even just for a moment. Though this can be hard to accept especially for people who are control freaks, you need to start surrendering to the uncertainty. Experiment with trying to let go of the need to control the present moment, the past or the future, and this includes controlling the people around you. If you can lean to your uncertainty and take the time to tolerate it, the less control it can have over you.

By constantly experimenting with the different strategies you will soon master over your anxiety.

Your first few tries won't bring much change as they're like drops of water in a bucket. Same thing will happen to the next, and so on. Things won't be noticeable at the start, but as you continue to use them regularly, eventually, you will be able to have more capacity to harness the strength of your wild but beautiful mind to make it work more in your favor.

You will soon realize and understand that you will always have what it takes and that your anxious thoughts and feeling will simply pass away like a bad weather day.

Chapter 3: The psychology of Vampirism

We all have needs. How we get to those needs is how we live. There is a universal knowledge that how we get our needs can be either positive or negative. We are all taking and giving in life. The paths of both dark and light do not move at the same speed.

When we think of a vampire, we think of a blood sucking fiend. An individual who tilts back the neck of some young girl and drinks from her. A wipe of excess blood is flicked from the mouth as the vampire takes the girl to death or close to death. The deep drink and the euphoria of someone's vibrancy and life-force entering the beast drives it to a state of ecstasy.

The girl slumps into a pile of mush.

The vampire glows with power sucked from the girl.

This is the vampire.

Much can be learned from this artistic representation of who we are. For we are all vampires and we are all little girls slumping into a pile of mush. It is just a matter of degree.

With the exception of the pure psychopath, there are no pure vampires, and even then, the psychopath has often been the little girl at one point in their life or another.

We all experience the range of existence that is the thing we call life and living. Living life is unavoidable. We all have to do it. It is how we get what we need from others that determines if we vamp or not. This is the dynamic of the practitioner of dark psychology. It is of course, a matter of extreme. The severity of the draw measures the severity of the darkness. It also is a measuring device on the technique of the draw. The technique of the dark.

We all get vamped. When you are around others, there is the potential of getting vamped. There are many, many ways to have essence drawn from you. From the physical exertion of a demanding physical act to the spiritual energy sucked from you to another. It is when this happens that we need to examine what is exactly going on.

The reward of the practitioner of dark psychology is a feed. It can be a feed as subtle as someone trying to figure out what it means to feel, or a feed from your money pocket book to theirs.

Joy is experienced when the darkness falls upon us. Not by the victim, by the practitioner. There is a gain when you get full. It is the type of gain that may never fill the hole of those who just take. There is a pride in taking. We have been that way for a very long time. Bravery is often described by taking. The taking of another tribe's livestock. The taking of a hill in war. The taking of everyone's money and making it your own. We have been taking from each other for as long as we have been wandering this rock called Earth.

Possibly longer than that.

There is a need to feed. We all get hungry, and our hunger drives us in ways that we often do not understand until we are very hungry. Is our pride and self-lost to hunger? This is the drama and joy of the dark vampire. When the self is lost to the hunger that is within, we begin to see a dynamic occur. That dynamic is the hunter and the hunted. The victim and the victor.

When we stand victorious over another, we have to look at the playing field. Was it a fair contest? What did we do to win? The drawing of something from another can come at a price. During our hunger we do not take the time to slow down and look at the price. That happens after the contest is over.

Some would say there is no such thing as fairness. That anything and everything needs to be done to win. When we look at life and death, we see that there are only two options. On or off. So, in getting our hunger to subside, and remaining on while others are turned off, is victory.

There is a cold harshness to this. That there is this absolute about death. When the vampire sucks another dry to the point of where we turn off, there is a chill. A lack of emotion or conscience or consequence often arises, and if we are lucky, we live long enough to see the universe play out. When we vamp, we end up giving into basic survival or pleasure emotions and we forget that there is a bigger picture taking place.

There is also something that happens when you feed off of another. There is a euphoria that takes place. Like a blood infusion that can make it so you can do things normal, uninfused humans cannot, a joy develops from the action. The feeding of life from one thing to another is a mastery of control. This control is a joyous thing in itself.

So, there is joy found in the taking of others. From pride and honor of the steal, to the infusion of life-force from one to another, we feel something in the moment. And then, if we have a conscience, we deal with the fallout after victory.

The other side of the vampire feed is the victim. There is something to be said for being drained. That in itself can be a euphoria. When one relinquishes control to another they no longer have to drive. It is a release. A vacation from yourself, easily given to another.

Often so easily, that we do not know we are doing it.

When we are sick, we try to expel all things that are not helpful. If we look at it as degree of being sick, we can feel the urge to expel. For example, when we have a stressful day and we do not want to deal with the realities of life anymore, we can escape that life by anything as drastic as infusing drugs, to something as innocent as going shopping.

We like to feed others. It makes us happy. It is shown over and over again that when you examine the dynamic of someone helping another, the person helping can get more potential benefit than the person being helped. Sound confusing? It is. Try this.

The euphoria shared by the vampire and its victim can be measured. The victim is feeding the vampire therefore helping them. The vampire gets fed to survive, knowing that killing its victim will end the source. The victim, knowing that they are the source, receives this power. The vampire gets to live. The victim gets to live. The vampire gains by receiving the infusion. The victim gains by knowing they helped, and yet are not reliant on the vampire to survive. However, and here is where the balanced becomes unbalanced, the vampire needs the victim.

The cost of the practice of the dark arts of psychology eventually make a vampiric dynamic so that the victim wins. Minus life being removed in the case of the extreme, when a victim falls prey to any form of dark psychology the immediate loss is evident and takes its toll. The end game is that the practitioner of the darkness cannot give and will eventually fall into their own trap and wonder why and how they lost all control and got there.

Everyone likes to escape themselves. Even the most self-loved individual needs some time away from themselves. We search out the vampire to escape ourselves. We like it. We crave it. We like to turn our necks and feed other humans and things. This is not a weakness. The true strength is in the giving. For when you take, there is only one conclusion, you are only receiving. When we are only on the receiving end we become incomplete, and are ultimately weaker than those who can do both.

So how do we help the vampire without destroying ourselves? This is an age-old question. The love for the dramatic darkness is inside us all. The severity of how we will take on that darkness is up to us to use judgements as to our strengths. The cold hard truth is that sometimes a vampire is just that—a vampire.

In the world of fantasy, the vampire cannot return to humanity. They are the living dead. The death is final and they are stuck.

We are not true vampires. We may have difficulty processing our conscience. Even though there are those who would argue that we are glued to our screens in a way that makes us the walking dead, we are not. Life can change. That is the purpose of us moving forward. To change to situations so that the positive moves forward and the negative falls into the past.

There is a simple litmus test on vampirism. We all want to help; it is in our nature to do so. And there is no real reason to not help the vampire. In other words, we need to help the dark.

The trick is to draw a line. This means that we have to know what our boundaries are. When the vampire pulls us out of a comfortable space into an uncomfortable one, we need to take a moment to examine what is going on. Some will make their lives so that when that uncomfortable happens, all stops. This is acceptable because when it gets boiled down to the most basic, we are the best judge of what we need.

When not just escaping from ourselves, and we need to help someone in the dark, we must be on guard. There is power in helping another. There is also power in seeing a situation for exactly what it is. There is a chess game being played by each side when we try to help each other.

To blindly play, is to ask for victimization. When we are the vampire we must play smartly, knowing that there is a price to pay for taking from another. When we are the provider to the vampire we must also play smartly, to preserve who we are.

Chapter 4: Manipulation and its Types

Manipulation is a strategy of organizing your options on the chessboard of life so that you are able to achieve your ultimate goal. It is about carefully engineering circumstances to work in your favor.

Types of manipulation

There are many different types of manipulation. The following are the most common

- Psychological manipulation

- Emotional manipulation

- Social manipulation

Social manipulation is group-based. It could involve relationship manipulation within a given group. Within social manipulation, we can have political manipulation, media manipulation, religious manipulation, military manipulation, etc. The primary agent of social manipulation is SOCIAL ENGINEERING.

In this Chapter, we are focused on individual manipulation and thus we are going to be chiefly concerned with psychological manipulation and emotional manipulation.

Psychological (Mind) manipulation

Psychological manipulation refers to altering someone's mindset (attitudes, beliefs, and habits) to achieve set objectives.

In this chapter, we are going to consider the key traits of psychological manipulators and the telling signs that you are being psychologically manipulated.

Signs of psychological manipulators

- They are expert victims – always crying foul and pushing you to apologize even when they played a role in the happenings

- They always tend to use love word as a tool to manipulate you – "if you really love me, then you wouldn't have done this".

- They will push you to question your sanity and thus leave you mentally and emotionally in disarray – they employ gaslighting.

- They always want you to be in their emotional and psychological terrain while they never genuinely make effort to join your own – for example, they narrate their predicaments to seek sympathy from you but they show utter disinterest in your own predicaments

- They play the silent weapon when you are emotionally loud – when something goes wrong, especially which they have contributed to happening, they play silent or cool such that you find yourself like the one out of your mind.

- They never show any sign of accountability for the emotional turmoil they push you in. For example, they will hurt you but never say sorry.

- They always endeavor to invalidate your feelings. Whenever you try to express your feelings, they quickly obfuscate them by substituting with their own feelings and thus making your feelings seem unjustified.

- Triangulation – they always endeavor to create a third dimension into a mutual relationship between two people with the aim of breaking it apart. In essence, they introduce their own emotional angle into the two emotional angles… thus triangulating it. Theirs is like a horn that gores the relationship apart. Triangulators are common in a relationship. It could be your friend who flirts and seduces your girlfriend or boyfriend and takes him/her away. They also exist in politics.

- Blasters – they explode at any mistake done. They yell, scream, and shout such as to drown your voice.

- Powerful dependents – these are people who feign weakness and pretend vulnerability so that they can extract care from those who are empathetic of their welfare.

- Feigns love and empathy

- Play the innocent card – pretending to be in utmost shock and confusion when accused of wrongdoing.

- Over-aggression – using anger outbursts to shock their victims into submission.

- Denial

- Spinning the truth

- Frequent mood swings – this keeps the victim off-balance

- Love-bombing followed by a sudden devaluation

How psychological manipulators go about carrying out their manipulative endeavor

The following are some of the typical ways by which psychological manipulators execute their game:

- Substitution of facts (creating alternative facts)

- Creating a home-court advantage

- Let you speak first so as to be able to establish your baseline and thus take advantage of your weaknesses

- Overwhelm you with facts and statistics (in essence, pushing you to their mental territory where you are weak)

- Overwhelm you with bureaucracy – complex and utterly irrelevant procedures

- Use negative surprises – for example, waiting till towards the tail-end of negotiations to introduce surprises that dilute that which is almost concluded.

- Making sure that you are almost time-barred in decision-making – so that you end up making irrational decisions

- Employ negative humor – with the aim of puncturing your self-esteem and self-confidence

- Persistently judging you negatively so as to make you feel inadequate

- Feign ignorance – especially where knowledge of facts is to their disadvantage

- Guilt-baiting – pushing you into situations where they can blame you, judge you negatively or push you to apologize and in essence, have a superior psychological position

- Playing victimhood – exaggerating issues so as to win sympathy or achieve martyrdom. Often, use a person sense of goodwill, responsibility, empathy, etc., so as to extract undeserved benefit or undue concession.

- Moving goalposts

- Non-committal

- Diversion of the conversation to avoid certain discussions

- Flattery

- Sarcasm

Typical traits of psychological manipulators

The following are some of these inherent traits in a typical psychological manipulator:

- Idea sower – subtly and passively keeps sowing new ideas which, in essence, are there to yield his personal benefits. He proposes the ideas, traps you into tending them, afterward, claims the fruits of it.

- Constant inquisitor – uses negative probes as tools of criticism. The main intent is to make you feel inadequate and the inquisitor superior.

- Selective listener – sieves through your words and thoughts only to capture that which he/she can use to manipulate you.

- Reverse psychologist – reverse psychologists try to dissuade you from doing that which they want you to do knowing very well that you are more likely to do it on that basis that they are dissuading you. Alternatively, they can persuade you to do that which they don't want you to do and verily know that you are not going to do it. Their main aim is to harden your position or reinforce it to their advantage.

- Constant victimhood – constantly plays the victim card, especially when she/he is guilty so as to scare away any potential consequences of accountability

- Masked braggart–employs subtle means to make you feel inferior. Uses a know-it-all approach and tries to mundanely corrects you even if it means trying to make his/her synonyms of your words appear more superior even though out of context.

- Projector – projects a certain kind of mental image in you such that it overpowers your very own mental image.

- Deliberate mis interpreter – they misinterpret facts to suit their own point of view. This could include playing with synonyms, antonyms, similes, proverbs, quotes, etc., to derive the alternative meaning of a given statement.

Emotional manipulation

Telling signs that you are under the influence of an emotional manipulator:

- killing with kindness

- convenient neediness

- projecting a calm, cool and collected composure

- always "just joking"

- they play emotional blackmail – "I can do nothing without you", "I will kill myself if you leave me", "I will die without you", etc.

- homing you (home-court advantage)

- Tugging on your heartstrings (it will be heartless of you to do this), "if you have a heart, please don't leave me alone", etc.

- Excessive compliments and flattery

- Excessive generosity

How to avoid being manipulated

The following are the general tips that can help you avoid all form of manipulation:

- Don't be afraid to say no

- Speak up and stand your ground

- Learn to read those around you:

    - body language – rigid, tense, and use gestures to distract

- body posture – power posing with the objective of dominating you

- eye contact – trouble making eye contact. Or if they do, you feel like it is piercing, and unnerving in terms of its duration and intensity

- voice tone – forceful (to dominate, especially by superiors), nervous (timid lie, especially by juniors), or modulated (in case of persuasion, seduction, etc.)

- Trust your intuition – the sixth sense can get you out of trouble or nasty situation. Intuition is inherently in us human beings as it is in all animals. It is largely a survival mechanism. We lose this ability when we fail to trust it. We gain it when we rely on it… it is susceptible to learned non-use.

How to Be Safe from Emotional Manipulation

There are several people who manipulate emotionally and are of different levels all within our midst. As young kids, we often think that some psychological pressures do not affect us. However, part of really growing up as a person will include comprehend how you are guided by the surroundings that have been influenced greatly by different people and even driven by your needs as an individual.

Since we share certain innate psychological features that make us vulnerable, we can all be manipulated to some extent. Just like it occurs with other weaknesses out there, there are people who are obviously likely to fall to these challenges, while there are also others who possess a high immunity degree to pressures and that would lead us into doing certain things, we are sure of doing.

Every emotion, whether bad or good, serve a great purpose in all our life journeys. Despite all that, we should be alert of some people who would want to apply the emotions' string power for manipulation us. If you are a typical empath, then this can greatly happen to you, since this classification of individuals is highly prone to getting negative energy from other people. Do you, at some point, find yourself being taken advantage of or have families and friends that confront you on the issue of being dormant? There are a number of reasons that people allow others within their circles to manipulate them. Some of these reasons include political correctness, emotional insecurity, or just a meager desire to please other people. But by directing your efforts only to things that you can easily control, you will be able to lower the chances of ending up being emotionally manipulated.

To prevent being manipulated mentally, here are the steps that you should follow:

Recognize the Manipulator's Signs

Make sure you are aware of the situation at hand – In most cases, mental manipulation is subtle. This implies that it can almost impossible to notice when it is occurring to you. But there are certain common features and actions that manipulators do most of the time. Some of these common things include making a person doubt him or herself, projecting insecurities, as well as casting doubt. Being aware of the situation at hand means you learn how to tune into the feelings of your situation. When you do, you will be able to spot any case of manipulation much easier.

The next time you feel that you are being manipulated, then there are things you should ask yourself if you are doing something out of your willing heart or you feel responsible, obligated, afraid, embarrassed, ashamed, or guilty. If there is something you are doing for any of the mentioned reasons, then it can be true that you are under mental manipulation.

Look out for people who threaten to take things away from you – The point here is to be wary of a person who threatens withdrawal. These are the kind of individuals who make you feel like they might withdraw certain things from you if you do not behave in a certain manner. This is outright manipulation. Such characters might include the withdrawal of many things including their support, money, love, or even company.

There is a group of people who are always motivated by this type of manipulation, particularly in workplaces. That's why you will see them working late since they are afraid, they might miss the next promotion if they don't put more effort. Unknown to them is that this trait can be very damaging in personal relationships between individuals. This is because such interactions usually include more intimate emotions.

Love withdrawal statement is so common these days. This is a case where one member of a relationship gives the other opportunity to do anything they desire, but no interactions later on.

Be wary of a person who makes you feel guilty – a manipulative individual will always try to make you feel the guilt of not doing what they need you to do. They can easily attain this objective by pretending that you are letting them down. Similarly, they can also initiate a discussion on how much of an inconvenience a certain situation or thing is for them.

In most cases, we encounter guilt whenever we feel like we are part of the bargaining team. However, in circumstances where a person feels that he/she is being mentally manipulated, you should try to recheck whether you agree consciously to some of the things that you feel guilty about or if the individual is just making you feel the guilt for no good reason. Guilt statements can be coined to appear like they are positive. Statements such as, "I thought you really cared for me" can be considered as guilt statements.

You should also watch out for individuals who make their problems more urgent than yours – Those who are manipulative usually achieve their agenda by ensuring that their own problems appear more pressing or more important than the others' problems. If you are in a position where you feel obligated to assist someone with something, then just know you are being manipulated.

Each time we choose the kind of tasks that are most important to finish up in our lives, we tend to organize them based on their urgency. However, when other individuals decide the urgency for a given thing, then it becomes not only manipulative but also very problematic.

Pay much attention to excessive application of figures and facts – You can also be manipulated by those who tend to spout out so many figures and facts. The main idea that lies behind this technique is to make a person feel as if they don't know just as much as the other individual. The person who does this is only interested in convincing you that they are superior to you in terms of intellect.

Be careful when a person refuses to talk – There are those who manipulate others by refusing to talk first. They can also do that by just offering a silent treatment. When a person does this, they may be trying to probe certain information that they might later use against you. Alternatively, the person may also give you time so that you speak first and find out what your goals are and what you think is happening in your life.

Take note of the volume of the voice of the individual – There are some manipulators who will speak so loudly or just shout to subdue their victims. They are the kind of people who will drown out your voice with their own so that you can cease defending yourself, and ultimately, give in to the demands of the other individual. If a person is speaking over you or yelling at you, then that becomes a clear case of manipulation. They may also try to use a number of other tactics to make sure that you are entirely subdued. Some of these tactics might include standing over you or even blocking your path.

Reflect on the times that the person has attempted to catch you off-guard – Manipulators can also try to spring things on you and use your lack of preparedness to their advantage. By catching you off-guard, the individual is hoping that you are more likely to give in to their request. A person who is attempting to manipulate you, for instance, will try to ask you a very important question when you walk through the door. They might also ask you to do a very important task within a very short or no notice.

What to Do when Being Manipulated

Here are some of the things that you can do when you have realized that some individual(s) are trying to manipulate you.

Think about the person(s) trying to mentally manipulate you – The first thing to inquire here is if it is one person involved or a group of people. If you are dealing with a group of people in your case, then it would be better to take the matter up with the leader of the group or the person that appears to be the weakest of them all. All you need to tell them is that you feel like they are giving you too much pressure and pushing you into doing something you really don't want to do.

Ask them some questions – The other important thing to do when you feel that someone is trying to manipulate you is to try and ask a number of probing questions. This is a way of catching them off-guard and also gives you the time to analyze the situation at hand and decide how you want it to be handled. Here are some of the questions that you can ask these people:

- Can I contribute in terms of ideas?
- Does this whole process appear reasonable to you?
- What do I stand to gain out of this?
- Are you telling me or asking me?

Decline the Request – When the individual who has manipulated you ask you to do anything out of your will, then just refuse. At first, this can be hard. The person will be very surprised at the moment you will offer no for an answer. The art of sticking with your NO is a critical part of not letting yourself to be easily manipulated by others.

Don't give in to Series of Attempts – The best thing to do when you are under pressure of being forced to perform a task that is not appealing is to say no and just walk away. You shouldn't allow an individual manipulating you to coerce you by giving you pressure severally. Just disappear from the situation if they refuse to accept your refusal.

Just confront the person – This can work best when done in a place that is private. You need to let them know that you don't intend to let yourself be mentally manipulated or controlled. You should, however, not forget to mention that you are not exiting the friendship, but the person has to fix his/her behavior first. This shouldn't depress you at all. It is very imperative to recognize the fact that this individual did not improve your life at all.

Don't Succumb to Undue flattery – One of the common methods that mental manipulators use is giving their victims unnecessary praises and flattery. When you are praised by an individual, particularly when you have not done anything to deserve it, you might feel good and even easily give in. However, that is just one form of trickery that is applied by a manipulative person who is fully aware of what they are doing. You should try to show them that you appreciate the compliment, even though you do not feel like you have done much to be praised that way.

How to Prevent Mental Manipulative Cases

Here are some of the ways that can really help when it comes to preventing mental manipulative situations:

Look carefully for the real causes – The first thing that you should ask yourself is if there are certain possible causes to your personal manipulation. Maybe, just saying no seems not to be that easy, or maybe you just feel sorry for some individuals. Either way, it is very imperative to dig deep into the main cause of the issue so that you can be sure that it does not happen to you in the future. There are times that people don't realize that they also play major roles in their manipulative processes.

Stay away from manipulative persons – If possible, stay as far as possible from manipulative people. Even though they might try to make you feel special, remember that you don't owe these people anything. You are very free to decide how you spend your time and the kind of people that you hang around with. As noted earlier, if you feel like someone is trying to constantly manipulate you, then the best thing to do is to avoid them at all chances. It does not imply that you have to bring your relationship or friendship to an end. All you need to do is to be more in control of how mostly you see people around you and in the circumstances.

Let your experience guide you in avoiding the mistake in the future – Learning how to discern the early indications of manipulative behavior is one of the best ways of staying safe. An individual like this, for instance, will always want to change the manner in which you appear. That's why they will always want to offer you suggestions as to how you should change your personality and looks. They will try to tell you what you should and shouldn't wear, and even how you should present yourself in public. They will tell you not to laugh aloud in public or wear certain clothes when going out. When you see these signs, just run for your life.

Seeking Help Outside

Get advice from a trusted friend – Speak to any family member or a trusted friend any time that you have the opportunity. But first of all, it would be very important to check the situation alone and analyze some of the behaviors that could have been happening between you and the manipulative. However, it is still important to get opinions from others, since they will offer you an objective viewpoint. It is common for an outsider to note things that you can't on your own since you are deeply involved in the whole thing.

Seek Counseling - At times, it becomes beneficial to get insights into our personal characters by discussing it with a professional who is trained in the therapy of the counseling sector. Seeking counseling can greatly assist when it comes to identifying the reasons why you make yourself manipulated, and some of the things you can do to change the case at hand.

Taking a break can also be important at times – If you are feeling overwhelmed by someone who is very manipulative, then the best thing to do is to take a break from them. Do not feel obligated to continue staying in relationships that put you through a lot of stress for no need. Just take a break.

Chapter 5: Persuasion vs Manipulation

Persuasion

When you hear the word persuasion, what comes to your mind? Maybe the advertising jingles of a product urging you to buy a pizza from them, or maybe political campaign slogans trying to convince you to vote for a particular candidate, or maybe a pushy salesman trying to sell you a car. You are absolutely right if you think those are acts of persuasion! Politicians, news, mass media, legal proceedings and advertising can persuade you and influence your decision making. Most people like to think that they are immune to such influences. But then most of us own Nike sneakers, Ray Ban sunglasses or of course the new I-Phone. So advertising must have played a role in influencing your decision. Persuasion is constitutional within human communication and social interaction. When communicating, wittingly or unwittingly, people are always supporting and/or promoting certain ideas and behaviors over others. Therefore, persuasion is intrinsic to social interaction and not a matter of choice.

The study of attitudes and how to change them can also be referred to as Persuasion. Most of the things that involve molding attitudes that shape our world, involve persuasion. It is through persuasion that positive changes can be brought to the society. It is persuasion that convinces motorists to drive sober and buckle up. It is persuasion that helps end wars and forge peace between nations.

Persuasion is a psychological technique of presenting arguments in such a way that motivates, influences, or changes a person's attitude, or behavior in order to achieve the desired outcome.

The main components of Persuasion are:

- Persuasion incorporates symbols, verbal and nonverbal, to change attitudes. For example, images like Nike Swoosh or Adidas Three Stripes; words like freedom and justice; nonverbal signs like Holy Cross or Star of David.

- Persuasion involves a conscious and thoughtful attempt to influence another person. The persuader is always aware of the potential susceptibility of the person to accept change.

- Persuasion is a voluntary act of changing our own attitude or behavior.

- Persuasion is completely driven by the science of communication and requires a relay of verbal or non verbal message to the persuaded.

- Persuasion of the self is at the heart of the art of Persuasion. People must always be free to decide if and how they want to change their attitude and behavior.

Manipulation

Psychological Manipulation can be defined as a way to influence people's emotions, attitudes or behaviors which is neither rational persuasion nor coercion. The term manipulation is inherently thought of as negative and involving an element of moral deprecation. Human beings are inherently gregarious which makes them influence one another all the time. Consider, the influence your older sibling had on you growing up. That is a classic example of "healthy social influence" and must not be confused with the dark act of manipulation. In Psychological Manipulation, the goal of the manipulator is always to influence their victim into fulfilling their own desires.

People often confuse "manipulation" with "influencing" but they are poles apart in practice. Starting with the intent and motive of the person; an influencer is often looking for your best interest and approaches you with advice on how to make a decision better; but a manipulator has the mindset of how can I control your thoughts and emotions to get a better decision from you for myself. Thus, understanding the motive behind any such behavior plays a pivotal role in deciding whether it is a situation of "influencing", "manipulation" or even Covert Emotional Manipulation.

Covert Emotional Manipulation

The most widespread form of manifestation of Dark Psychology in today's world, which after reading this book you might agree with is Covert Emotional Manipulation (CEM). Now you are probably thinking is that different from Emotional Manipulation and if so, how. The answer is Emotional Manipulation occurs within the realms of your consciousness, so you are aware that someone is trying to appeal to a more generous side of you to get what they want. Think about the time when your parents wanted you to visit them for the summer but you had a different probably more exciting summer plans with your friends or a special someone and your parents insisted you visit them instead or take some extra time off to make the visit. You tried to convince them that you would visit for Thanksgiving and your calendar is booked solid and they might have retorted with statements like "we are old and we wouldn't be around for so long, you need to make us your priority" or "we haven't seen you in forever and we miss you, come over to visit your loving parents". During this conversation you are completely aware that your parents are attempting to change how you feel about your summer plans in their favor. This is a classic and harmless case of Emotional Manipulation. On the other hand, Covert Emotional Manipulation is carried out by individuals who are trying to gain influence over your thought process and feelings, with the means of subtle underhanded tactics that go undetected by the person being manipulated.

By definition Covert Emotional Manipulation goes undetected and leaves you acting like a pawn in the hands of the manipulator, which makes this a manifestation of Dark Psychology. The dictionary definition of the word covert is "not openly shown or engaged in", therefore, it presents a stark difference from all other Emotional Manipulation techniques. The victims of Covert Emotional Manipulation are unable to understand the intent or motivation of the manipulator and the way they are being manipulation and even just the fact that they are being manipulated. Think of Covert Emotional

Manipulation as a bomber with impeccable stealth, one that can tip toe in your subconscious without being detected, leaving you with no defense what so ever. Our emotions primarily dictate all other aspects of our personality and thus they also dictate our reality. Someone attempting to manipulate your emotions is equivalent to them cutting open your jugular vein making you lose control over yourself and your reality.

The many differences between Persuasion and Manipulation

Motive/Intent

As we have established people with active dark psychological traits including manipulators, aim to establish control and authority on their prey and exploit their victims to serve their own interests. On the other hand, persuaders are concerned about the wellbeing of their audience and attempt to convince them to change their attitude or behavior in a free environment.

Method of Delivery

Manipulators create an inviting environment for their victim, who is often an unwilling prey and primed emotionally and psychologically to act in ways that benefit their predators and threatens their own health or well-being. Whereas, persuaders only hope that their audience will respond to their influence and the suggestions. Ultimately the individual is free to decide whether or not they want to accept the suggestions made by their persuader and alter their thoughts, feelings and/or behaviors.

Impact on the social interaction

Dark manipulators will always aim to isolate their prey from the rest of the world and prevent any contact from their loved ones. The victim of dark manipulation like brainwashing, develop extreme views and may commit heinous acts of antisocial behavior. Unlike manipulation, acts of persuasion are never lethal for the audience and the society. It could be as harmless as your brother's admiration for Nike shoes leading you to buy a pair of your own or the ads from McDonalds inviting you to enjoy a quick meal with your family.

Final outcome

Persuasion usually result in one of these three possible scenarios: Benefit to both the persuaded and the persuader, commonly known as a win-win situation; Benefit only to the persuaded; Benefit to the persuaded and a third party. However, dark manipulation always has a singular benefactor that is the manipulator. The manipulated individual is at grave disadvantage and will act against their own self-interest.

To drive this difference home, let's consider this example. Brian is on a budget and walks in the store looking to buy a new Smart TV. He is greeted by Adam, who then proceeds to show him all the Smart TVs available in the store. Adam explains to Brian all the unique features of different models and says: "So and so Samsung model is little over your budget, but it is the hottest product on the market with the best audio and video quality and is worth going over your budget". Now,

If Adam truly believes in his recommended TV model and has the best interest at heart for his customer. That's definitely act of Persuasion. On the other hand, if it so happens that Adam's recommended is not really worth its high price, but that sale would make him extra commission, so he convinced Brian into buying a bad product at high cost. That's manipulation!

Chapter 6: Manipulation by lying

Lies is defined as the act of hiding the truth, especially to get an advantage. It is further related to words such as hypocrisy, half-truth and even perjures. Another definition describes it as a dishonest or illegal method used to get something or make people believe that something is true when it is not.

Lies is also considered a form of mind control due to the effect it has on its subjects. Lies can involve a lot of different things including sleight of hand, propaganda, dissimulation, concealment, camouflage and distraction.

Lies can be very dangerous because the subject or affected person is made to believe something that is a lie or usually very different from the truth. It could even be a piece of information that can keep the subject out of harm's way.

Lies is seen often in our daily lives. In families, relationships or even in the work environment. It leads to mistrust and sometimes betrayal, which damages the relationship between the people involved. This further leaves the affected person with security issues, as they won't have the sense of security that they are used to. Imagine being lied to by the person you feel is your closest friend, partner or spouse—the damage is never easy to repair, if there will ever be a repair. When lies occurs, there has been a violation of the relational rules and can make it difficult for the partner to trust the other for a long time.

Often, lies happen for different reasons. Sometimes it is to hide the truth from someone we love, other times to hide a mean idea or opinion of others. No matter what type of lies or reason for it, a lot of people do not find it easy to handle and many find it hurtful.

There is a common saying: "Hurt me with the truth but never comfort me with the lie." Most people feel the need to hide the truth because they feel the subject cannot handle the truth, but it is not your place to determine what a person can handle or not. This is a common mistake made by people and if this mentality is kept there will always be cases of lies.

Lies can also occur in different levels and spaces. White lies are not meant to harm but could still fall in as lies. Most people prefer this method when trying to relate an unpleasant raw truth, as it is an easier way to relate information.

Have you ever considered an online dating service? This is also another place where lies are common. There is a higher likelihood of men giving a false representation of the assets they own and the goals of their relationship while females are known to commonly misrepresent information like weight and age.

Self-lies is also a popular thing these days. An easy example is procrastination. This is a situation where you make promises to yourself about certain goals but are unable to accomplish them. You are straddling in the worlds of manipulative lies and white lies.

Another type of lies is known as mendacious lies, which occurs when deceivers show conscienceless behaviors and act with the intention to cause stress and harm to others. Paradoxical defenses are used by these deceivers for blaming others for what they are also guilty of in order to diverge them off the point. Ponzi schemes are typical examples of this kind of scam, and this kind of lies might end up resulting in an evil lies.

Evil lies, in simple terms, are intended to bring fatal harm to its victims. They are shown via oppressive actions. Agents of lies that practice this are the paradoxical defense gurus. Positive labels are also used for instance the democratic actions society, to hide ulterior motives. These evil lies spread through different movements and are usually known to start with an enticing promise and end in destructive dictatorships.

According to interpersonal lies theory, there are 5 different types of lies that are found. They are:

Equivocations

This also contains false information as the agent of lies. With equivocations, the information given is contradictory, ambiguous, or indirect and cannot be comprehended by the victim. The victim tends to get confused and is unable to understand what is going on.

This technique is usually used by the agent to avoid a situation where the victim returns with blame for the false information. The agent of lies can outright deny it because no information was given if you think about it.

Concealments

This happens to be one of the most common and frequently used types of lies. In this type of lies, the agent omits relevant information, especially things relating to the context, intentionally. The agent may conceal information that is important to the subject. There is no direct lie here. However, the important and useful information that is needed by the subject will not be given.

Exaggerations

This is when the agent overstates or puts so much emphasis on a fact and adds more to the truth than there is to make a story more interesting or to have the story turn out the way they would like it to be. Like concealment, there is no direct lying going on here. However, the situation being talked about will often seem like a bigger deal than it really is. Sometimes, there are changes to the truth and this is done so that it will appeal to the subject.

Understatements

This is the direct opposite of exaggeration. It involves the agent downplaying or reducing aspects of truth to the subject. They will make the topic feel as though it is not much of a big deal or like it really doesn't matter. When, in fact, it is something that the person needs to know. It might be information that could be a stepping stone to the person's dreams or the sole information the person needs.

Understatements can leave room for the agent to return from an experience where they did something wrong but look as though they're innocent in their version of the story.

When caught understating events, the agent will often act like they did not realize or even know the information was important or meant anything to the subject. Anyone who listens to it will feel like the victim is being so hard on the agent of lies here, but the agent only played the right cards and can look good in the end. However, by that time the damage will have already been done.

These are some of the methods used in the act of lies. For a person to be completely deceived, at least one of the given methods must have been used. Looking at these things, it is going to be difficult to tell if you are being deceived or not. Often, the only way you can know if you are being deceived is if you already know the truth before a person tries to deceive you.

How to Spot Lies

In order to identify lies, it is a good idea to learn about how to detect when lies is going on. It tends to be easy if the agent of lies slips a little by mentioning something, which you already know to be a lie, something that you are completely sure cannot be the truth. Also, sometimes the agent of lies starts to contradict what he/she must have said before.

As difficult as it might be to keep up with a lie for a long time, it tends to be very easy for people who know each other well. A person who knows you well can easily tell how to pull one over on you.

Whenever you have a feeling that someone is trying to deceive you, it is required that you pay a lot of attention. This is because it takes a toll on the agent of lies who is trying to keep up with lies, which are sometimes interwoven, all to avoid a situation where he/she will slip up about something they have already said or lied about. Due to this, the agent might in one way or another leak out certain information that will tip off the subject, either through nonverbal or verbal cues.

According to research carried out, the process of discovering lies is usually cognitive, fluid and complex, and will vary from time to time based on the message that is being passed. So, is detecting lies impossible? No. But is it difficult? Yes, it is.

Investigators have tried and have not succeeded in identifying a cue (verbal or nonverbal) to easily detect lies. Spotting lies now relies on several cues with changing percentage of predicting lies successfully. Certain clusters of verbal and nonverbal displays should be identified in order to raise the likelihood of detecting a liar, and these displays have to be compared against an established baseline which must have been identified during a period when the agent of lies had little or no reason for lying.

Basically, there are little signs that might be signs of lies, some are nonverbal which you might be able to see. Body language tells a lot. However, you should also consider that the person might just have those physical tics normally and it might not be related to what is going on, such as nervousness or shyness.

Here are some verbal and nonverbal cues that may indicate lies:

- The agent of lies answers questions that were not asked.

- Questions are usually answered with questions.

- When mistakes are made, self-corrections are usually avoided so as not to give the idea that they are unsure about what is being said.

- Some common phrases like "I don't know" or "I can't remember" are always employed to make it look like they forgot.

- Liars often talk about what they did not do, as it is easier to keep those ones real as compared to what they did.

- When a person is lying, there is always a justification for their actions, even in situations where justification is not necessary.

- A person who wants to be deceptive can go as far as including times and dates just to prove that they are innocent of the offence in question.

- In order to hide the truth, liars often use fewer words to describe the subject or activities being talked about.

- A liar is usually passive in terms of language when describing events or activities.

If a question is asked and the person is reluctant to answer directly but engages in some form of interference, develops a poor structure of logic, repeats certain words a lot or talks faster for one question, these are signs that the person could be lying. But again, these verbal and nonverbal cues should be used with caution as researchers are yet to figure out an actual cue to detect lies.

Remember that liars are very good at saying or doing things that will make them look as truthful as possible. Even truthful people end up saying or doing things that may make them look deceptive. Detecting lies is not impossible but at the same time it is not easy.

In the lies process, it can be very difficult to determine which factors show, but there are components that are very typical or common that you can observe during this process. You might naturally not observe these factors unless the person has told a big lie that you are conscious of.

There are three main factors to be discussed when it comes to lies. These are camouflage, disguise and simulation.

Camouflage

Just as the name implies, it is used by a person to hide the truth by using half-truths in a way that the person getting the information will not feel like anything has been left out. The truth of the matter being discussed will be given but not in detail, so the person being deceived here has no idea that some information is being left out and might not realize this until the issue is finally brought to light and when all the truths have been established.

Disguise

This involves a complete representation of what you are not. The agent of lies, in this case, tends to play a role that he/she is not, thereby creating a new identity that cannot be linked to the actual self. This is really damaging because it hides the true nature of what is going on.

Disguise can occur in different ways, like the agent of lies hiding a variety of information such as his/her name, the kind of job they do, their purpose for being at that place and even the purpose of having a conversation with the victim. When this occurs, the victim is left vulnerable to attacks, as they have let themselves fall for the new persona that the agent has adopted and are likely to release more information than what would be given if they knew the truth about the person.

Simulation

This is just a direct way of showing the subject information that is false. Simulation can be done through mimicry (depicting something like themselves and claiming the credits), fabrication (depicting an event that is not real or did not happen and making it a cover story for themselves) and distraction (making the subject of lies focus on something else rather than the truth in the information being disclosed).

Defenses Against Lies

It is relieving to know that there are defense mechanisms against lies and a person faced with a deceptive situation can always stand against and defend him/herself from it.

According to researchers, pride was one of the major factors that allow people to fall into lies. When a person feels he or she is too good and perfect, or feel he/she can be very careful, then it leaves room for the con agent to take advantage.

Enlightened skepticism is a technique used to defend yourself against lies, there is a saying: "truth fears no questions." This approach protects you from harmful forms of lies, as it is a way to assess the truth through a fact-finding and questioning method. When you do these things, you tend to gain from this effort in at least three ways, which are:

- You tend to hone your critical thinking skills.

- You learn to choose who to trust and to what extent to trust them.

- You get to find out who is after personal advantage at your expense.

In order to risk falling into someone's deceptive trap, researchers have come up with some enlightened skepticism questions that can help you to defend yourself against lies.

Some of the questions to ask include:

1. What are the things I know about the person's truthfulness?

2. Is the person's statement consistent with the truth or reality?

3. Is there a way to verify or check the authenticity of the statement?

4. What do I stand to gain if I accept and act on the statement?

5. And if I don't gain, what would I lose if I accept and act on the statement?

6. What is the gain of the speaker if I buy into the statement?

7. Is there any part of the statement exaggerated or downplayed by the speaker?

8. Does the idea seem or sound too good to be true?

9. Would I advise my close relation to accept the statement without an iota of doubt?

10. What doesn't feel right?

These 10 questions make you more objective and allow you to think critically when receiving information. When you ask and answer these questions there is a lesser chance that you will be fooled since you will come across as sincere and sharp and this will ward off deceivers as they will move on in search of easier targets.

Just like simulations occur in lies, there is also simulation in defending or warding off the lies.

These lies detection skills come with some fun simulations, some of which includes:

Talk shows on TV

Listening to people argue about different topics. Pick out the truth, the exaggerations and half-truths told by a speaker in the process of making his/her point. Also, look out for outright lies, emotional reasoning, fallacies and all other deceptive behavior. Being able to identify these things allow you to get better at detecting lies.

Commercials

These also gives you opportunities to work more on your critical thinking skills. In advertisements there are a lot of mistakes in reasoning, arguments based on things without facts, a lot of lies and lies. Being able to detect this will improve your ability to detect a deceptive person from a distance.

If you can find the flaws in simulated information, hold on with judgment until you have enough information to render a reasonable accusation. It is only at this point that you can say that you have truly mastered the act of deceptive defense.

But again, a person who is good at defending him or herself from lies is only as good as the agent of lies he/she is faced with. Some people tend to be more skilled at lying and constant interaction and simulation are the only way to improve on one's lies detection.

Chapter 7: Dark psychology and Control of Power

Power isn't coercive and regards the privilege of the individual to pick and to acknowledge or decline the proposed conduct. In power, it might appear to be externally that the individual is permitted to choose. Notwithstanding, under the shallow misrepresentation of the opportunity of decision, there is an undercurrent of passionate compulsion.

The procedure of passionate control includes two gatherings: the controller and the controlled in the process of power, which has its very own elements.

The Manipulator:

Controllers lie on a range of various characters. They are altogether described by variation from the norm in nature. It is anything but difficult to recognize the heartless, unfeeling, insensitive, and callous insane person. Nonetheless, some other cluttered characters may utilize control to endure their pathology and keep up their mental uprightness. A sincerely dependent individual may look for his enthusiastic needs by controlling others. The equivalent with the narcissistic character when somebody has a go at satisfying their desire for power, prestige, vanity, and self-magnification by controlling others. The theatrical which is looking for attention, extravagance, fulfillment of shallow enthusiastic and sexual needs may utilize all their tempting and emotional embellishments to control others. Individuals with Borderline character with their confusing feelings and feeling of inward void, emotional episodes, rash undertakings, and carrying on will control others even by their hatred or self-hurt.

The controller attempts to control the controlled to keep up his enthusiastic or individual increases. A few controllers can without much of a stretch move their concentration starting with one unfortunate casualty then onto the next yet others my battle as far as possible to hold their injured individual under their hooks.

The Manipulated:

Few out of every odd one can be effectively controlled. This is consistent with some degree, even though an astute insane person can threaten the least powerless by strategies of dread.

The most helpless against control are those serene and hesitant people who lack fearlessness. They are generally honest, accommodating, fair, or once in a while, guileless. They might be forgotten people, damaged and looking for shelter in the hands of the reliable controller. They may lack confidence, with a profound feeling of blame, which is scanning for discipline and an inclination that they should have the right to be rebuffed.

Indeed, even the individuals who can intellectualize their life problems may mislead themselves by working their mind hard into the shrouded justifiable explanations behind the controller to act along these lines. They discover excuses for the culprit, yet they disregard excuses to liberate themselves from the hands of the controller. They appreciate intellectualizing their enduring as they find out confronting their powerlessness too excruciating to even think about living with.

The Manipulation Process:

Various strategies are utilized in the control procedure. Some are plain, and others are too unpretentious to even think about exploring or too complex to also consider analyzing.

1. Instillation of Guilt:

Blame is a substantial negative spark. Controllers know by experience that their exploited people can feel regretful effectively. They see that the injured individual even admit his shortcomings and apologizes and feels humiliated pointlessly. Steadily, they make the unfortunate casualty accepts they are bad enough, they couldn't care less enough, or they are egotistical, brutal, exploitative, and even parasitic. Indeed, as a rule, the controller has a large portion of these highlights. The unfortunate casualty can not look judiciously to see this isn't accurate because he/she has been modified into self-question, self-fault, and admiration of others together with devaluation of self.

2. Disgracing:

A controller uses strategies to make the injured individual feels despicable, dishonorable, and insufficient so that there will never be a way out. When the unfortunate casualty attempts to challenge a controller, the last makes the injured individual feels embarrassed by terrorizing, dread, blame and self-question, with an allegation of lack of capacity to do anything, lack of stamina, of power or mental fortitude. Mockery, jokes, criticism, and negative remarks, or even just dangers might be utilized. Once in a while, the controller incites the unfortunate casualty into a demonstration of hostility out of dissatisfaction and agony. This usually neglects to free the person in question. In any case, the controller would utilize such occurrence to make the unfortunate casualty feels further disgrace, disappointment, and blame.

3. Picking up Sympathy:

The controller may play the job of the unfortunate casualty to pick up compassion and collaboration if different strategies fall flat. Summoning empathy, pity, and kindness from somebody honest aren't troublesome in that capacity people can not stand seeing somebody who is enduring or in agony. The controller continues bemoaning how unfortunate they are, the way unreasonable things are, and how they are casualties of such coldblooded life.

4. Terrorizing:

Dangers might be unmistakable or clandestine. A scary look, disregarding the other individual, articulation of displeasure or objection are a portion of the creepy demonstrations. At times, it is faking rage and a blast of feeling which is utilized to threaten the individual into accommodation. Dangers may go from outrageous conduct to destroy the economic wellbeing of the unfortunate casualty up to physical assaults and now and again dangers to execute.

5. Enchantment:

Sexual control is utilized to give a misguided feeling of closeness and guarantee the obligation of the relationship. Passionate temptation by honeyed words, acclaim, and enchanting disposition can be quickly used to make the unfortunate casualties bring down their safeguards and addition their trust. This usually is brief and flighty, and through such irregular uplifting feedback, the injured individual is guided into the round of control.

6. Lying:

Lying is at the center of control either by retention a lot of reality, excluding some significant certainties, or manufacturing false stories. The controller may overstate or limit actualities, cheat and hoodwink the person in question and construct an incredible picture of himself, his unfortunate casualty and their relationship. Faking is another type of viable lying. The controller may deny that he has done anything incorrectly purposefully or that he was unconscious of the impact on the person in question or may put on a look of amazement or resentment. Distinct lying through denying "what you are discussing?" or claiming to be distracted or confounded is once in a while utilized. Faking sickness or pain, fainting or false fits might be used to pick up compassion and debilitate the safeguards of the person in question.

7. Justification:

The controller may utilize various moves to clarify the explanations behind his conduct, which use the powerlessness of the person in question. If the unfortunate casualty is guileless or unfit to pass judgment on a contention fundamentally, the controller may utilize a large number of the misrepresentations of rationale to beat his injured individual's counter-contentions. When the unfortunate casualty is ridden with blame, disgrace or brutal soul, the controller uses all contentions which advance to such vulnerabilities.

8. Refusal:

The controller may obtusely deny any wrongdoing or decline to let it out or dodge talking about the subject inside and out. He/she may participate in a drifting, superfluous befuddling talk which may redirect the attention to a shocking matter. Refusal is unique about lying if the individual is unconscious somewhat or entirely of reality.

9. Anticipating the fault:

The controller may extend the responsibility on the person in question, blaming him for his very own considerable lot indecencies or at times denounce other people who have wronged him for a mind-blowing duration and who made him what he is. The injured individual may feel either blame, or he is put on edge to account for himself, or he may feel compassion and distress for the controller.

10. Hostility:

The controller may depend on real hatred and brutality to cause the injured individual to submit to his will, specifically if the unfortunate casualty is flimsier or crippled. This may leave an unexpected in a faked upheaval of indignation or extreme anger. Any reaction of a comparative sort from the injured individual is looked with increasingly intense animosity which might be later accused on the unfortunate casualty himself, or a created disease might be charged with just ascribed to the enthusiastic issues the controller professes to confront.

Chapter 8: Tactics to Manipulate Others

When it comes to working with dark manipulation, there are going to be a lot of different methods and techniques that we are able to use in order to get what you want. Remember we are talking about some forms of manipulation that are going to help us to get what we want but may end up harming the other person in the process. This means that they may not be seen as the best options to work with, and you may feel a bit uncomfortable with them if you have not worked in dark manipulation, or even with dark persuasion, in the past.

However, working with these techniques will help you to get the results that you want. They will ensure that the other person you are using as your target will be likely to do the actions or say the things that you would like them to, even though it may not be in their best interests to do so. With that said, let's take a look at some of the different dark manipulation tactics that you are able to use to get someone else to do what you want.

Using isolation to get what you want

The first technique that can be used in mind control includes isolation. Humans are very social creatures. They like to spend some time talking with others, spending time out in public, having close friends, and family, and spending their time in more social situations. When we take this social aspect away from many individuals, it changes the way that they look at life.

Complete physical isolation can be the most powerful. This is when the subject is taken away from all contact with others, including email, social media, phone calls, and physical contact. This is something that has been seen in cults and with other groups. They will often take the person far away from others, and then the only human contact that the person can have is with the captors.

Now, this total physical isolation can be really hard to do, and it is usually only done in really intense situations. If you are just trying to use manipulation, you usually don't want to go through and completely isolate the target. But it is common for a manipulator will typically try to attempt their target mentally as much as possible.

There are a number of methods that the manipulator can use in order to get what they want with the help of manipulation. They could include some seminars that last a week in the country and isolate the person from what they would usually do. They could be a lot of criticisms of the person family and close friends so that the target feels bad and stops seeing them. It could be jealousy that keeps the target at home and limits the amount of influence that anyone outside the manipulator has on the person.

Once the manipulator is able to control the information that goes to the target, they can share information, withhold information, and do anything that they would like in order to continue influencing the target as much as they would like. The target is going to become reliant on the manipulator, and this is how the manipulator is able to work and get what they want from the target. There are no outside influences to tell the target that something is wrong, or that they should watch out, and this ensnares the target even more.

Criticism

The next option to work with when it comes to manipulation is the idea of using criticism. This one is sometimes used with isolated or on its own and it works well because it makes the target feel like they are always doing something that is wrong, and that they are not able to meet the high standards of the manipulator. The criticism can always show up on a variety of topics and could include how they look, who they hang out with, the clothes they wear, their beliefs, and anything that the manipulator thinks will work for this.

When a manipulator decides to use this tactic, they are going to be really good at hiding it behind one of their compliments to the other person. Or they will say something nice and add this little jab at the end of it. This allows them to say all the mean things that they want, and then they can say that the target misheard or misunderstood them and that they hadn't really meant any harm by it. This puts the target in a bad spot because they know the manipulator is being mean to them, but they are the ones who look paranoid and bad in this situation.

The criticism that the manipulator is going to use is often going to be small. They don't want to start out using really big criticisms that are obvious because the target doesn't want to be criticized. If the manipulator starts out with something big, the target is going to fight back and walk away. But when it starts out small with some little comments along the way, it starts to plant a bit of self-doubt, something that the target is going to notice, but they often are not going to fight back against.

They are going to start out with something that may seem like a compliment or like that is going to sound like they are being helpful, but in reality, they are trying to be hurtful in the process. They may say something like, "I didn't know that you liked the color blue. I think you should go with something else." This one is going to have the hidden meaning inside of it that you don't look good in what you are wearing, and your clothes don't look that well.

Or maybe you bring in your favorite outfit to a meeting to make yourself feel better. You are excited and you feel really good about the way that you look and feel in the outfit. But then they are going to say something about how they liked you in some other outfit better. It isn't necessarily mean, but it is said in a manner and at a time that it ends up hurting your feelings in the process.

As time goes on, the type of criticism that is going to be used against the target is going to get worse. And the criticism is going to become quite a bit more obvious as well in order to add in a bit more self-doubt here. This is going to make it so that the target starts to rely on the manipulator a bit more. This is due to the fact that the target is going to feel like they have so many flaws that are hard to ignore, and that the only person who can like them and maybe even loves them, through these flaws will be the manipulator. The fact that the manipulator is still around is a good sign that they care, and this causes the target to be more willing to do what the manipulator asks.

The manipulator is going to find that they are able to use this criticism more of us against them kind of idea if it works better as well. They could even choose to move their criticism to be against the outside world so that they can claim they are more superior.

When this happens, the manipulator is going to claim to their target that they are super lucky that the manipulator is even associating with them. The manipulator will ensure that they are important so that the target is more likely to stick around and do what they want. This alone is meant to be enough if it is done in the right manner so that the target feels lucky just because the manipulator is going to spend time with them.

Alienating the target to get what they want

No one wants to be alienated. They want to feel like they are a part of the group. They want to feel accepted, as they belong, and more. This is never more apparent than when we see a newcomer. When someone is new to town, or to school, to work, or somewhere else, you will notice that they are trying to figure out how to join into the group and get them to accept them. They are worried that they are going to be alienated, and in order to avoid this, they will do everything in their powers to get others to like them and go along with them, and this is where the manipulator can come in and get what they want.

Newcomers who start to join a new manipulative group are usually going to receive a welcome that is very warm. And they will form a number of new friendships that seem to be much deeper, and have a lot more commitment and meaning behind them compared to anything that they were able to experience in the past.

There are several reasons for this one. First, this gets the target to feel welcome and more indebted to the group, and the manipulator. They are thankful that they have these deep connections, and it is usually easier to get a friend to go along with something that a stranger, so it works to the benefit of the manipulator as well. Add in that the target is scared to be alienated, then they are going to do what they can to keep the relationships going strong.

If there are any doubts that end up arising, later on, these relationships are going to become a powerful tool to ensure they stay with the group. Even if they aren't completely convinced, the target will start to remember their outside world, the world that they had before joining this group, and it is going to seem cold and lonely. They will instead choose to stay with the group, even if there is some manipulation going on.

Simply because of the fact that we do not want to be taken away from the crowd and we don't want others to have anything to do with us, we are going to do what the manipulator wants us too. The fact that humans are very social creatures and like to be included in some kind of group all of the time, it is likely that we are going to give in to these urges to do what the manipulator wants, even if we don't feel like it is the best thing for us.

Using social proof as a form of peer pressure

As we talked about a bit before in the last section, we like it when we are able to be a part of the group. Sometimes we center this around wanting to fit in, and we will follow the rules and do what we can to make sure that we are liked and part of the group. And even when we are more introverted and don't want to be in the group all of the time, we still want to find a group of people we are able to be around and fit in.

The thing is that the manipulator is able to come in here and use the idea of wanting to fit in to help them work against you and get you to do things that you don't want to. They know how much fitting in is going to matter to you as an individual, and they are going to use this to convince their target that they need to act in a certain manner if they want to be able to fit in with others.

When a manipulator wants to work with a group of people with the help of this tactic, such as when you have a cause and want to get some people on your side, then you will use what is known as social proof. This can be almost like brainwashing and can help make it so that the people in the group are going to assume that the actions that others around them are using are the right ones, so they should follow it as well. This is the idea that if everyone else is doing it, then the actions are going to be really justified and it is fine for you to do them as well.

The thing with this one, if the manipulator is successful with what they are doing, then the action that they suggest is not going to matter. This is why it is common for us to find someone who separates out from the group doing actions that may not be seen as acceptable by the rest of society. This can work well any time you are able to find an individual who is feeling some kind of uncertainty about their lives or about what they should be doing. They are going to look around for some guidance on what they should do, and if the manipulator is able to get ahold of them during this time, they are more likely to get their target to go along with whatever they want.

Repetition

This one is going to use the idea of when we do something a bunch of times, it becomes more likely that we are going to get that to turn into a habit and stick. And this is a way that a manipulator is able to control their target. If the manipulator is able to repeat the message over and over again, and they use the same tools when repeating the message, they are more likely to get what they want.

Constant repetition can be a powerful tool of manipulation. It seems like a simple idea but it is going to be really effective. The more times that you are able to repeat your message to the target, and the more you keep things the same each and every time, the more likely it is that they are going to end up doing what you would like.

Fatigue

This method is going to take advantage of someone when they are tired and worn out. When we haven't gotten a lot of sleep recently, and we feel worn down, our decisions are not always going to be the best. Think about how a new mother is going to feel when she is trying to take care of a new baby and hasn't been able to get a lot of sleep done in the last few weeks. Manipulators are either going to wait until their target hasn't been able to get a lot of sleep naturally to ask for something, or they are going to be the ones who create this kind of environment so that the target is low on sleep and energy.

You will find that this can be effective because often we do not have to go for a very long time without sleep before our brains start to go foggy. This is a bad thing when you want to be able to protect yourself from those around you and you want to make sure that you are not manipulated. But for the manipulator, this is really good news.

How much sleep deprivation is required to make you feel groggy and tired and will affect your decision-making abilities? According to the Journal of Experimental Psychology, it only takes 21 hours straight of not getting enough sleep before we become more susceptible to the suggestions of others.

This is less than one night of sleep. Many of us have missed this thanks to catching up with work, cramming for a big test, trying to binge watch our favorite shows, staying up with a child who is sick, or for some other reason. Think about how much we have been influenced to do things during that time, and how much worse it could be if someone who was studying and using dark psychology came onto the scene at this time.

While it may not be the best news for your target, it is great news for you. You just need to either force a situation where the person doesn't get a lot of sleep (perhaps take them out for a night on the town and not let them get home before they need to go to work the next day), or wait until you hear they have had a long night and didn't get a lot of sleep. Either way, it is going to end up benefiting you. Once they have missed even one night of sleep, though more is often even better, then you are going to be able to see the results and can start to manipulate them without as much effort.

Working to form a new identity in the target

This one is going to take a bit more time to accomplish, and it is not something that you will want to work with if you only plan to work with the individual for a short amount of time. But if you really want to make sure that you are able to manipulate your target as much as possible, and you want to be able to come back to them over and over again to do this, then working on them and helping them to form a new identity may be the option for you. This is something that only skilled manipulators are able to do, but it is going to make a big difference in how you connect and interact with the target.

In this case, the manipulator wants the target to stop being themselves, and they want them to become a robot, someone who is willing to just mindlessly follow their orders. Using all of the methods and the different techniques of mind manipulation that we have talked about in this guidebook, the manipulator is going to try and extract a confession from the target, some kind of acknowledgment that the target believes the manipulator is a good person and doing a good thing. Of course, there can be some slight variations to this, but it is pretty much the same idea no matter how this form is used.

At the beginning of this technique, it may be something that seems pretty insignificant. The manipulator may be trying to get the target to agree that the other members of the group are fun and loving people. It could be the manipulator trying to get the target to agree that at least some of the manipulator's views are valid.

This may seem like a pretty simple thing to work with, but it is priming the target to start thinking with and agreeing with the manipulator on some things. Once they can get the target to agree with them on some of the little things, it is much easier to get them to move on to some of the bigger things. Before you know it, out of the desire to be consistent with what you do and say, you would then find that the target starts to identify themselves as one of the group.

These are just a few of the methods that you are able to use when it comes to working with manipulation in your own life and making sure that you are able to get the target to do what you would like. You will find that manipulation is often going to be a bit darker, and maybe even a bit eviler than the other two methods that we will talk about in this guidebook, and sometimes they may seem a bit advanced for the work that you want to do.

The good news is that as you progress through with dark psychology, you will find that a lot of the techniques that are used in manipulation are going to be very helpful to you when you want to be able to get your way. if you are stuck with some of the other methods that are available, or you find that they are just not cutting it, then using some of the techniques that we have talked about in this chapter are going to be the best option to help you out.

Of course, before you start to use them, consider whether you have formed the right connection with the target ahead of time or not.

There are a lot of things that can go wrong when you are using these more advanced techniques, and if you try to use them too early in the process, or before you and the target are ready, then they are not going to work well for you. Once you do the analysis and make sure that you are set and ready to really use them properly, the techniques of manipulation that we have talked about in this chapter are going to prove to be valuable.

Chapter 9: NLP

Neuro-Linguistic Programming has to do with the study of thoughts (neuro) and language (linguistic) in a systemic way and the scripts that run the life of an individual (programming).

It deals with the understanding and the development of the mind and the entire understanding of the language of the mind in relation to the way it is designed to function and the ways in which it is molded by the personal experiences of an individual. It is simply a study of a person's subjective reality.

A proper understanding of the language of the mind influences every aspect of a person's life from his relationship with others to his communication skills with friends and clients to the general outcome of a person's life. It is a holistic study that puts the spirit, body, past and present of an individual into consideration.

As homo sapiens who are gifted with the ability to think, it is presumed that our most important function is the thought or the thinking function. NLP, however, brings one to the understanding of the fact that no thought process exists in a vacuum, as they are a product of a person's perspective. It has a presupposition of perception as reality and it holds that the things, we think are colored by the way we think.

For different individuals there are different ways of thinking and interpreting reality. What NLP does is assist in the understanding of these various representational systems to help each person narrow down his own system. It helps in the understanding of the three different types of thinking patterns which are:

- **Visual:** deals with both pictures and visual metaphors.

- **Auditory:** sound (hearing).

- **Kinesthetic:** deals with the five senses, as well as gut feelings.

In NLP, a person is thought to take absolute control of his mind and ultimately his life. Unlike what is obtainable in psychoanalysis, which places its focus on "why," NLP presents a more practical approach with its focus on the "how."

The Origin of NLP

Here is one thing that has not been highlighted in this article – that neuro-linguistic programming is a science. It was a science that was invented in the 1970s by two main Californians, John Grinder, and Richard Bandler. At that time, John Grinder was an associate professor of linguistics at a university that was known as UC Santa Cruz. Bandler, on the other hand, was a student at the same university, before later becoming a mecca for radical thinking and psychedelics. Together, these two great innovators worked together to model the techniques that had earlier been given by Milton Erickson, a professional hypnotherapist, Virginia Satir, who was a family therapist, as well as the founder of Gestalt therapy, Fritz Perls.

Both Grinder and Bandler sought to reject a number of what they had witnessed as the ineffectiveness of talk therapy. Instead, they opted to go straight into looking at the technique that was used to the behavioral change. Bandler was a major in computer science, and they were both inspired by the revolution that had been created by computers over that time. So, they opted to create a psychological programing language for people.

What this duo came up with was a type of evolution of hypnotherapy. Whereas the classical hypnosis fully depends on certain methodologies to place put patients in suggestive trances, neuro-linguistic programming is way much less heavy-handed. It is a system that is used to lay certain meaning into both written and spoken language so that it becomes easy to plant suggestions into the unconscious mind of an individual without them realizing what you are doing.

Even though mainstream therapists refused to apply the techniques of Neuro-Linguistic Programming terming it as pseudoscientific nonsense, it was still able to catch on despite all that. It can be remembered that the Human Potential Movement was still in full swing back in the 1970s, but that didn't stop neuro-linguistic programming from spreading all across. Bandler would later make more than $800,000 from this great creation and was even being booked for various trainings in various departments. As of today, the main techniques of Neuro-Linguistic programs, as well as the Ericksonian-type of hypnotic writing, have spread the world over.

How NLP Works

If you are just coming across this topic for the first time, NLP may appear or seem like magic or hypnosis. When a person is undergoing therapy, this topic digs deep into the unconscious mind of the patient and filters through different layers of beliefs and the person's approach or perception of life to deduce the early childhood experiences that are responsible for a behavioral pattern.

In NLP, it is believed that everyone has the resources that are needed for positive changes in their own lives. The technique adopted here is meant to help in facilitating these changes.

Usually, when NLP is taught, it is done in a pyramidal structure. However, the most advanced techniques are left for those multi-thousand-dollar seminars. An attempt to explain this complicated subject is to state that the NLPer (as those who use NLP will often call themselves) is always paying keen attention to the person they are working on/with.

Usually, there is a large majority of NLPers that are therapists and they are very likely to be well-meaning people. They achieve their aims by paying attention to those subtle cues like the movement of the eyes, flushing of the skin, dilation of the pupil and subtle nervous tics. It is easy for an NLP user to quickly determine the following:

- The side of the brain that the person uses predominantly.

- The sense (smell, sight, etc.) that is more dominant in a person's brain.

- The way the person's brain stores and makes use of information (the NLPer can deduce all this from the person's eye movement).

- When they are telling a lie or concocting information.

When the NLP user has successfully gathered all this information, they begin to mimic the client in a slow and subtle manner by not only taking on their body language, but also by imitating their speech and mannerisms, so that they begin to talk with the language patterns that are aimed at targeting the primary senses of the client. They will typically fake the social cues that will easily make someone let their guard down so that they become very open and suggestible.

For example, when a person's sense of sight is their most dominant sense, the NLPer will use a language that is very laden with visual metaphors to speak with them. They will say things like: "do you see what I am talking about?" or "why not look at it this way?" For a person that has a more dominant sense of hearing, he will be approached with an auditory language like: "listen to me" or "I can hear where you're coming from."

To create a rapport, the NLPer mirrors the body language and the linguistic patterns of the other person. This rapport is a mental and physiological state which a human being gets into when they lose guard of their social senses. It is done when they begin to feel like the other person who they are conversing with is just like them.

Once the NLPer have achieved this rapport, they will take charge of the interaction by leading it in a mild and subtle manner. Thanks to the fact that they have already mirrored the other person, they will now begin to make some subtle changes in order to gain a certain influence on the behavior of the person. This is also combined with some similar subtle language patterns which lead to questions and a whole phase of some other techniques.

At this point, the NLPer will be able to tweak and twist the person to whichever direction they so desire. This only happens if the other person can't deduce that there is something going on because they assume everything that is occurring is happening organically or that they have given consent to everything.

What this means is that it is quite hard to make use of NLP to get other people to act out of character, but it can be used to get a person to give responses within their normal range of character. This may come in the form of getting them to donate to a charitable cause, or finally making the decision they had been putting off or getting them to go home with you for the night if they had considered it at some previous point.

At this point, what the NLP user seeks to do may be to either elicit or anchor. When they are eliciting, they make use of both leading and language to get the person to an emotional state of say, sadness. Once they can elicit this state, they can then lead it on with a physical cue by touching the other person's shoulder for example.

According to theory, whenever the NLP user touches the person's shoulder in the same manner, the same emotional state will resurface if they do it again. However, this is only made possible by the successful conditioning of the other person.

When undergoing NLP therapy, it is very possible for the therapist to adopt a content-free approach, which means the therapist can work effectively without taking a critical look at the problem or without even knowing about the problem at all. This means that there is room for privacy for the client as the therapist does not really need to be told about whichever event took place or whatever issue happened in the past.

Also, prior to the commencement of the therapy, there is an agreement which ensures that the therapist cannot disclose any information, hence the interaction between the therapist and the client remains confidential.

In NLP, there is the belief in the need for the perfection of the nature of human creation, so every client is encouraged to recognize the sensitivity of the senses and make use of them in responding to specific problems. As a matter of fact, NLP also holds the belief that it is possible for the mind to find cures to diseases and sicknesses.

The techniques employed by NLP have to do with a noninvasive, medicine-free therapy that enables the client to find out new ways of handling emotional issues such as low self-esteem, lack of confidence, anxiety and destructive relationship patterns. It is also a successful tool in effective bereavement counselling.

With its roots in the field of behavioral science, which was developed by Skinner, Pavlov and Thorndike, NLP makes use of the combination physiology and the unconscious mind to bring about change in the thought process and ultimately the behavior of a person.

The Importance of NLP

Neuro-Linguistic Programming is not only necessary for the understanding of a person's being, but it also helps in the understanding of the way an individual is. It helps a person to get deep into the root cause of the problem, as well as the foundation of their being.

It helps people take responsibility for the things that they feel they may not be able to control. With the help of NLP, it is possible for a person to change the way they react to events of the past and have a certain level of control over their future.

It is very important for people to be aware of the body language of the members of their inner circle, as well as those who they seek to do business with. With NLP, it is possible to make use of language with both control and purpose, and with this it is possible to have control over your life. Remember, you cannot expect to make the same mistakes using the same mindset and hope to get different results. During an NLP session, the focus is placed entirely on the client as they are made the subject. This helps a lot because at the point where a person can deal with his or herself as a person, they gain more clarity into his or her dealings with other people.

It helps to improve finance, sales performance, marriage, health issues, parenting, customer service and every other aspect and phase of life. This is because it helps in the holistic improvement of an individual and when a person is whole, his interactions and relationship with himself and other people become whole as well.

It assists in targeting your beliefs, thoughts and values and helps with the targeting of a person's brain functions, as well as developing certain behaviors. It also shapes the way these behaviors metamorphoses into habits and how the habits change to actions which in turn comes as results.

Manipulating the Mind with NLP

As you may already know, there are several techniques that can be employed when it comes to the subject of mind control. For the purpose of this book, in this section we are going to focus on the ways in which the mind can be manipulated with the use of NLP. The following are a few of those ways:

Close attention to the person

When a person is trying to manipulate another person's mind with the use of NLP, they do so by first paying close attention to the subtle cues of the person like breathing pattern, body language, pupil dilation, eye movement, nervous tics, body flush and so on. Thanks to the fact that the emotions of a person at a time are easily linked to such cues, it is easy for the NLP user to infer the person's state of mind.

Also, the NLPer notes these gestures in order to be able to determine the ways that a person perceives and processes every piece of information. For example, if a person is asked about the color of their favorite shirt and they move their eyes to the top right corner, it becomes obvious that they have visually created their answer. Similarly, if they move their eyes to the top left corner, it means that they have created a visual remembrance as they flash back to the color of their shirt.

In recent times though, studies have shown that this technique is not very reliable as it has to do with so many other factors that make it more complicated (Praveen, 2016).

Talking with a suggestive frequency of the human mind

This has to do with the uttering of words close to a person's heartbeat, which typically is about 42 to 72 beats every minute. When this is done, it can induce a high state of suggestibility to a person's mind.

Moving past the conscious mind with the use of voice roll

This is a manipulating technique that has to do with voice roll, which is a patterned pace style that entrenches a desired point by skipping a person's conscious mind and going to the subconscious mind. An NLPer does this by placing emphasis on the word they desire the receiver to hear in a patterned style of monotony.

Building rapport easily, in secret

This is a manipulative technique used by the skilled NLP user. It is done by employing language to boost suggestibility. To create a rapport with a person, the NLP professional examines the person closely and pretends to adopt the person's body language in a very subtle manner, thus making the person more vulnerable to everything the NLPer suggests.

Programming the mind in a sublime manner and creating an anchor

This technique has to do with a process of creating an anchor in a person such that it becomes easy to put the person in a particular state of mind by simply tapping on the person or touching them in order to program the person's mind in a sublime manner.

Using hot words in an effective way

NLP professionals can adopt a pattern of words that may seem normal on the surface, but in truth they are permissive and suggestive. There are some hot words that are connected to the senses, these are the ones that are more suggestive. They include words like eventually, feel free, see this, means, hear this, now, because, as, etc.

These words are very potent in invoking a state of mind like experiencing, feeling, imagining, etc. It also creates the perception that the NLP user desires in the mind of a person. Also, they can make use of some vague words to control a person's thoughts.

An interpersonal subconscious mind programming

By making use of the interpersonal strategy, the NLP user can say one thing, when they are planting something else in the subconscious mind of their subject.

Protecting Oneself from NLP Mind Control

Many times, whether you are conscious of it or not, people will try to use NLP mind control on you to have you become submissive to them. This will include those you work with and those you get into intimate relationships with. Though, developing a keen and potent immunity to it will be of much help to you.

To do this, you must closely study the mechanics that are employed by experts in the field. Jason Louv (n.d.) suggests the following as ways of protecting oneself from NLP mind control:

Be very wary of those who copy your body language

When you are talking to a person that you suspect may be into NLP and you note that they are trying to copy some of your gestures and mannerisms by either trying to sit the way you sit or trying to place their hands the way you have placed yours, put them to test by making a few adjustments to the way you sit by changing the way you have placed some parts of your body to see if they will do the same.

For those who are skilled in the art of NLP, they will find it much easier to mask this than those who are new to it, as the new ones tend to copy the movement of the body almost immediately after you do so. When you notice such mirroring of your gestures, it is time to raise a point of order to let them know that they are beginning to cross the line.

Make random unpredictable patterned movements with your eyes

You will find that this is a very funny way to troll NLPers, but for what it's worth you should try it out, especially when your rapport with the NLP user is at its initial stage. At this stage, they will generally try their best to pay keen attention to your eyes. You may be deceived into thinking that their attention to your eyes is because they have an interest in what you have to say.

Maybe they are interested in what you are saying but this is not because they are interested in your thought process. The attention they give to your eye movement is because they want to study and know the way you store and process certain information.

Watching the movement of your eyes will give them certain information about you, such that in a few minutes, they will be able to easily decode when you are not telling the truth and even the part of the brain you use whenever you are speaking. This will give them so much insight into what your thoughts are, such that they will even appear to have some psychic information about your core thoughts.

To break this, you can begin to dart your eyes around whenever you speak with people that you suspect of using NLP so that you frequently look up, down and sideways. You can make it look as if this is a natural thing for you to do when you talk to people but at the same time, try to do it randomly without a pattern. This will make the NLP user go crazy as you will be doing so much to throw their calibration off balance.

Avoid being touched by anyone

This may be an obvious practice, but it should be done with more caution when you are having a conversation with a person whom you suspect may be into NLP. This is an especially important practice whenever you find yourself in a heightened emotional state of anger or laughter or anything like that and the person you are having a conversation with attempts to touch you at a point when you are still in that state.

For example, they may choose to tap you on the shoulder. If they do this, they would have successfully anchored you so that if they desire to make you go back to that state later, they can just touch you on the same spot. This is as suggested by NLP's wayward logic.

Beware of vague language

One of NLP's core techniques, which it adopts from Milton Erickson, is its use of vague language to initiate a hypnotic trance. Erickson discovered that the vaguer the language, the easier it is to lead people into a trance. This is a result of the fact that the person has less information to disagree with or even react to.

On the other hand, more specific language would easily take a person out of a trance. Take note of the language of politicians. For instance, Obama's "change" mantra is a good example of this technique, as the word is so vague that different people can easily read different meanings to it.

Pay attention to permissive language

Be wary of those that are prone to use such permissive phrases like "feel free to relax," "you are welcome to look at my new apartment if you like," "you can have it for as long as you like," etc. This is an early indication of a pre-NLP hypnotist like Erickson himself.

The best way to have someone do a thing or two, or go into a trance, is by making them give you permission to do so. This is true because a skilled hypnotist will never go the route of commanding you straight-up to do their will. You will never hear them say things like "go into a trance," but you will often hear them say things like "you are free to relax as much as you want."

Beware of gibberish

Pay keen attention to people who make phrases that may not really make sense when you pay close attention to their words. Gibberish is the core factor of both the pacing and the leading phase of the NLP. The hypnotist is not actually saying anything, what they do is to shape your emotional state in such a way that it moves you to the place that they want you to go.

To counter this, you can always ask them to be more specific about what they are saying or to explain what they mean by what they have said. What this does is to throw their technique off balance and ensures that the conversation goes in a specific order, with a specific language by breaking the trance. This includes the use of vague language that we discussed earlier.

Always read between the lines:

Those who use NLP will always use words or phrases with some hidden or covert meanings. On the surface their language, when heard quickly, will come across as though it is an obvious statement that you do not have to think deeply about before agreeing with.

For example, if a person says "diet, nutrition and sleep with me are very important things, don't you think?" you may, on the surface, agree with the fact that diet, nutrition, and sleep are indeed important, and it is a good thing that the person is paying attention to their health. So, without paying attention, you have already agreed with them but what about the layered message which lies in the phrase "diet and sleep with me." Without knowing it, you have already agreed to it. This is a very subtle art that is common with skilled NLP users.

Maintain your attention

You need to be careful when you are around NLP users to ensure that you do not zone out around them. This means that you must go into every interaction with them with a conscious cue.

For example, if an NLP user is trying to get you to work for them for free, the moment they notice that you are not really paying attention to them, and have begun to zone out, they will begin to use the technique to tell you about how lucky they are to never have to pay for any service because they always get people to do it for free. They will ensure that they ring this keyword into your head in order to change your mindset without you knowing it.

Try to not agree to anything

If you find out that you have been put under pressure to make quick decisions and it begins to feel like you are being steered in a certain direction, try your best to leave the situation. Give yourself time, wait as long as 24 hours or more if necessary before you make any decisions, especially ones that have to do with your finances.

Be careful to not be swept up to the point where you must make decisions based on your emotions in the spur of the moment. This is a common tool in the hands of salespeople who are always armed with different NLP techniques with the aim of making you buy on impulse. Always have it at the back of your mind that you do not have to do what they want you to do. Take a walk, breathe and make use of your rational mind.

Always trust your intuition

This is the basic, most important rule. Whenever you feel like a person may be messing with you or when you feel uneasy with a person, trust your gut feelings. NLP users will always seem off and dodgy. Stay as far away from such people as you can or be clear about the fact that you demand that they respect you enough to not apply NLP techniques whenever they are communicating with you.

As annoying and pernicious as NLP can be, it is possible to resist this modern day "black magic." You will always come across NLP users in different areas of your daily interactions. You may not be able to avoid them if you listen to politicians, interact with marketers or even when you walk into a used car sales lot. Arming yourself with this list will help you to avoid their gimmicks. You will be surprised at how much more aware you become of their techniques.

Practical Uses of NLP

When it comes to interpersonal relationships and interactions, NLP is a very strong and potent tool that could be useful to you in making those far-reaching changes in your life. There are times when we find ourselves asking several questions regarding the sensitive topic of NLP. One of such questions is how NLP can be of help to a person's life.

While there are several ways in which NLP can benefit a person's life, here are a few of the ways we can use NLP to our own benefits:

Getting the things you want

It is completely normal for a human being to set certain goals for themselves, as this is the only way in which a person can grow and attain new heights. These goals may be new goals for one's health, finances or even free/leisure time.

While some people only set goals at the beginning of the year, others learn to review their goals more frequently to set new ones by revisiting them on a monthly or quarterly basis. There are those who even set goals for themselves in a weekly or daily basis.

Regardless of what goals one may have set or who the person setting the goal is, there is one thing that is sure, it isn't very likely to reach all of one's goals. The best thing to do in this regard is to learn to increase the number or the percentage of the goals you achieve. It will certainly make a lot of difference to know that you can set a goal and know that you can achieve it. Therefore, what NLP does in this aspect is to help you master the ways in which you can use all the resources at your disposal to achieve your goals.

Persuade other people without them knowing

At times, you find yourself in situations or conversations where you are trying hard to convince others or trying to get them to understand you or see things from your point of view, but they just seem to be unwilling to budge in their position in the matter. Whether it is a case of you trying to persuade them or merely trying to change their notion of things, it is often almost an impossible thing to do.

With the help of NLP, you can understand the way they process information by paying close attention to the subtle cues that easily indicate the way they think. This will give you an upper hand whenever you get into conversations where you must convince people. All you need to do is to make some slight changes in the way you talk to them. This will not only make the interaction easier, but it will also increase your chances of getting them to see things from your point of view.

Know what motivates you and understand yourself

Have you ever stepped back to think about the reason why you react to things the way you do? Or have you ever thought about the reason why you do things the way you do? From all indications, what a person does and how they react to things can be predicted when they are able to figure out the things that make them thick.

The good news is that it is not difficult to figure out these things. The way a person behaves and the way they think are a product of the things they have experienced over time. There are a lot of ways that a person can make use of NLP to get a better understanding of themselves.

This can be done easily by getting to know how you process information and the kind of stories that you tell yourself, as well as the manner with which you retain the memories of past events. Getting an understanding of these things will help you to get control of them.

NLP helps you to be comfortable in new situations

It is not abnormal to experience a certain level of discomfort whenever you enter a new situation or territory. Whether you are travelling to a new city, picking up a new job or getting to know your in-laws for the first time.

Any type of new situation at all has the potential of stressing someone out and many people do not reach their full potential when they are stressed out. Since underperforming isn't much of an option, you can think of ways of handling new situations with confidence with the knowledge that all the resources required to succeed are at your disposal. This will help in calming your nerves and help you be less anxious.

The fact that you know that you will be able to handle whatever life throws at you is enough to make you relaxed. Thus, getting quality knowledge of NLP tools will help you discover that the new situations you are facing are not in any way different or less comfortable than the activities you take on every day.

Allergies

Allergies are a basic part of the daily lives of so many people. Although it may be annoying, it is an unavoidable aspect of life. Whether you are allergic to a certain common food or you seem to get allergies at certain times of the year, everyone will agree with the fact that life would be so much easier if allergies did not contribute to the already numerous troubles in life.

Chances are that you have already tried many medications and treatments. Now, imagine how great it would be to not have to carry a sanitizer with you everywhere you go or that your child can finally have that puppy you have long denied them for fear of it making your eyes water.

One of the first things that NLP is known for and what led to its popularity is the allergy process. Although the allergy process is not a cure, it offers ways to help you to reset your immune system. What it does is help you program your immune system so that it understands the things that are dangerous to you and the things that are not.

When you can walk through this process, you will be able to enjoy the freedom that you admire in other people. Your days will be free from the burning, itchy eyes you have sadly become used to. The sneezing will be subdued, and you will finally experience the comfort that you have not felt in many years.

NLP Techniques

Here are some of the techniques that are employed in the users of NLP:

Dissociation

Everyone experiences a bad day when a situation ruins it and gives one a bad feeling. This may be an experience that drowns your spirit every time you are faced with it. Also, it may be a certain nervous feeling that comes at any point that you have to address an audience. It could be a feeling of shyness that comes whenever you need to approach a certain (special) person.

Although it may seem as though this feeling of shyness, sadness or nervousness is automatic and unstoppable, what the NLP technique of dissociation offers are ways to get over these feelings.

To do this, you can:

- Get to know about the emotion that you wish to overcome. Whether it is a feeling of discomfort, anger or dislike for a certain situation.

- Imagine the possibility of teleportation and looking back at yourself going through the same situation, but this time from an observer's point of view.

- Take note of the dramatic change that occurs in the feelings.

- To get an extra boost for your morale, think about floating out of your body and watching yourself. This means that you will now be looking at yourself while your other self is also looking at yourself. What this double dissociation attempts to do is to take away all the negative emotions in all possible minor situations.

Content Reframing

This technique is useful for all the times you feel like you are trapped in a negative or helpless situation. With the help of reframing, you will be able to get rid of all negative situations by becoming empowered by interpreting the meaning of the situation into becoming a positive thing.

Take a situation where your relationship ended for instance. Although it may seem as if it is an awful situation when one looks at it on the surface, what about the possibility of those hidden benefits of being single? Think of the fact that you are now open to meeting and interacting with new people, which means that it is possible for you to get into a new relationship. This means that you are now free to do whatever you want to do at whatever time you want to do it. From the last relationship that ended, you must have learned some valuable lessons that will eventually be useful to you in your subsequent relationship(s).

All these are possible ways to reframe an experience. If you can reframe the meaning of the breakup you have just had, you will have changed the narrative and given yourself an entirely different experience of it.

It is very possible to panic or get thrown into fear in certain situations. Instead of focusing on fear, you can sway your focus by reframing. This will contribute to helping you make some even-handed and responsible decisions.

Anchoring yourself

This is a technique that was developed by a Russian scientist, Ivan Pavlov, who conducted experiments with dogs through the consistent and repeated ringing of bells whenever the dogs ate. After he had rung the bell repeatedly, he found out that the dogs started salivating every time they heard the bell. This also happened at times when there was no food present.

This process of creating a neurological connection between the ringing of a bell and the attitude of salivating is known as a conditioned response. These responses to stimulus anchors can also be used on humans.

The result of anchoring oneself is that a person gets to link a desired positive emotional response with a specific sensation or a phrase. When you can select a positive emotion or a thought and intentionally link it to a gesture, you will be able to trigger the anchor at every point you feel low, so you will be able to change your feelings immediately. Here are some ways of anchoring yourself:

- Take note of the feelings you want to experience. It could be a feeling of happiness, confidence, calmness, etc. Decide on the part of your body where you would love to place the anchor. This could be a certain action like pulling your earlobe, squeezing your fingernail or touching your knuckle. With this physical touch, you will be able to trigger the desired positive feeling whenever you want to. This has nothing to do with the part of the body that you have chosen, all that needs to be done is create that connection between the unique touch and the feelings. You do not have to make this touch for anything else besides the feeling.

Think about a certain time in the past when you had the same feelings you are experiencing at a given moment. Reminisce on the time you felt the same way then float into your body by looking through your eyes so that you will be able to replay and relive the memory.

Once this is done, you can make some adjustments to your body language to match with the memory and the state of mind. When you are reliving the memory, make sure you can see, hear and feel everything the way you remember it. If you can do this, the feeling will come back, just as it will when you tell a funny story from the past to your friend.

Keep in mind that you will typically begin to laugh over again as you tell the story because while you get into the story, you will create some mental association to the story and relive the experience.

While you are going back to this memory, pull, touch or squeeze that part of your body that you had earlier chosen. If you do this, you will notice that the feeling will heighten while you are reliving the memory. Once the emotional state gets to its peak and begins to wear off, you can then release the touch.

This touch will create a certain neurological response that will be a trigger for the state whenever you touch that spot again. So, in order to feel this state again, all you need to do is to touch yourself again in the same way.

To get an even stronger response, you can think of another memory from the past where you had that same feeling and go back and relive it from your own perspective. Anchor that same state as you have done before. Every time you add another memory, this anchor will gain more potency so that it will trigger an even stronger response.

Whenever you feel the need to change your mood, you can revisit this technique.

Creating Rapport with Other People (Getting Others to Like You)

This is an easy and common NLP technique that also has the strength to help you get along with almost everybody. There are so many ways that you can boost and create rapport with someone else and NLP is one of the quickest ways of building doing that.

It simply has to do with mirroring someone else's tone of voice, body language and even words. People find it easy to like those who are like themselves. With the subtle mirroring of someone else, the brain can fire off some neurons and pleasure sensors in the brain. This will make a person to automatically develop some form of admiration for anyone that is mirroring them.

This is a simple technique to adopt. All you must do is to stand or sit the same way the other person is standing or sitting. Also, you can tilt your head the same way the other person is tilting his and smile the way they are smiling. Mirror their facial expressions and cross your legs the way they cross theirs.

Also, imitate their voice and every other thing that you can imitate in their gestures. The best way to do this is to create a rapport unconsciously by adopting a subtle approach. If you are doing too much in the way you are associating with them, the other person may take note of what you are doing, and this will be a red flag and it will likely break the rapport. All you need to do is to remain natural and calm at the same time.

Influence and persuasion

Although almost all the work that concerns NLP has to do with ways to help people to get over any form of negative emotion, limiting one's beliefs, conflicts and bad habits, there is also another part of NLP that has to do with how to influence and persuade other people in an ethical manner.

Milton H. Erickson, who was one of the earliest mentors of this field, was schooled in the area of the subconscious mind using hypnotherapy, which is the real scientific aspect of hypnosis, as opposed to the entertainment hypnosis that is common in stage shows.

Erickson was so keen on hypnosis that he came up with a way of speaking to the subconscious mind of others without really making use of hypnosis. He had the skill of hypnotizing other people whenever and wherever in everyday conversations and interactions. This method of hypnosis is what was later known as the conversational hypnosis.

This later became a very powerful tool that was used to easily persuade and influence other people. It is used to help them overcome their fears, limitations and conflicts without them being consciously aware. Also, it is important when interacting with those that may be resistant if they become aware. You may want to think of those teenagers who may not want to listen or pay attention.

Chapter 10: Defensive Maneuvers

Believe it or not, there are ways to give yourself the most obvious opportunity with regards to not turning into the following measures in the neighborhood wrongdoing figure index. Give yourself the edge, remaining sheltered as you venture out around taking care of your business or public activity. Pursue a couple of essential personal safety tips, and you increment your shot of remaining safe. Figure out how to shield yourself the savvy way, wherever conceivable.

Walk upstanding and glance around as you stroll along, be alert. If you look exchanged on and mindful, odds are you will be disregarded. They will search for a more straightforward objective.

Tune in for clamors close to you, e.g.: - individuals approaching you, and it most likely is an honest individual simply continuing ahead yet you know!

Attempt to abstain from tuning in to your iPod or Mp3 particularly around evening time, how might you know when you have hindered your hearing and consideration redirected somewhere else. Also, the perils of vehicles and so on.

It is a great idea to have a cell phone with you, however, don't to have a long discussion about whether genuine or stage figured out how to attempt to show individuals you are associated. Again, this occupies your consideration away from remaining mindful.

At the point when at all conceivable always tell family or companions where you are going and what time to expect you back, this isn't as specific individuals assume an attack of your security. Its fundamental safety common sense.

Always stay where individuals are near and in all around lit boulevards, Avoid going down back rear entryways or worthless modern domains, you get the image. Counteractive action is number one when figuring out how to shield yourself.

When you believe you are in risk of being pursued, go to the closest entryway. Thump hard and yell, clamor and consideration are the last things a future mugger or attacker needs.

Never go to the place of an individual you have recently met, meet in an unbiased spot where individuals are near, and you are remarkably unmistakable. Become more acquainted with them first and see the location they give you is their first home. Perhaps request a telephone number and check it in the book.

Most importantly, don't place yourself in potential threat. If you need to hang tight for a companion or relative to join you, at that point pause and be sheltered, it is vastly improved than winding up on a real existence bolster machine or more regrettable.

When somebody in a vehicle stops to ask headings, don't go up and put your head somewhere around the window. Remain back and glance around to check whether a conceivable second individual is near. This could be a diversion robbery endeavor, again whenever assaulted make as much commotion as you can.

At last, if you are defied, and requested your handbag, cell phone, or wallet. The best thing here is to toss the article they need to the side and behind them. This will give you essential seconds to perhaps flee and raise the alert.

You may much consider conveying a subsequent wallet or handbag, with an outdated Mastercard in it. Also, a little money to look genuine. All the above are reasonable and useful ways to remain safe, as you travel around doing your everyday business. This is the ideal way to figure out how to guard yourself, continuing caution, and staying away from a showdown.

Defending Yourself From an Attacker

1. Fighting should just be utilized if all else fails. First attempt to prevail upon the assailant if that is conceivable. If they have a weapon and all they need is cash, its either conceivably your life or $50. Because you may realize how to disable an aggressor, does not imply that you might most likely damage everybody every time. You may have an off day, or you're drained, and after that, you mess up the opportunity to incapacitate the aggressor, and afterward, you get cut or perhaps killed. So at the end of the day, it is a lot more secure

to give the assailant what they need, when they have a firearm that would be your best alternative.

2. If the aggressor won't stop, then you should be prepared to safeguard yourself. First, you have to know about your environment consistently, so by this point, you should know where everything is around you. You have to get into a battling position with both of your hands up to square assaults. When you have your hands down, or in your line of vision, then you won't most likely square or divert the attacker's charges. Returning to continually monitoring your environment, it is a lot more secure to keep an article in the middle of you and your rival, for example, a refuse can and so on whatever might associate with you to prevent your aggressor from getting a straight line of assault on you.

3. Know how to square and strike proficiently. I can not pressure that it is so imperative to figure out how to hit your assailant in essential spots, for example, the throat, ears, eyes, sunlight based plexus, crotches, or knees. If your assailant is coming directly at you, and you don't have the foggiest idea what to do complete a speedy yet fantastic kick to within the aggressor's knee. Regardless of how vast the aggressor is, if you strike his knee super hard, at that point his establishment

will be disabled. No aggressor will be stressing over securing their knee, so you will quite often have that opportunity. Likewise, you NEED to realize how to BLOCK or at least DODGE. You would prefer not to be hit during an assault, and that is the place blocking or avoiding comes into spot. For instance, if they throw a jab, you can square and parallel advance to the outside of the punch. When you are outward of their punch, you are in the predominant position in light of the fact that your body is confronting them, yet they are not facing you which means in the event that they hit you that they won't most likely produce loads of intensity, However you will almost certainly since you are as yet confronting him and ready to strike the kidney's, ribs, or sanctuary. Parallel developments will be your best choice to evade an assault and put your body into an overwhelming position.

4. Know to make an appropriate clench hand and how to get control into the majority of your strikes. When you throw a right hook, you should just hit with your forefinger's knuckle and your center finger's knuckle, this reduction the possibility of you harming your hand because your clench hand is currently aligned with your lower arm. Additionally, you have to get your entire body into an assault. When you throw a right hook with just your arm, it won't be that incredible, in any case when you get your hips and middle into the punch, at that

point without a doubt your assailant will be harmed. If you toss a knee to the crotch or face, you should shoot your hips straight into the assault with your knee rather than merely raising your knee and hitting. This will guarantee that your aggressor does not have any desire to continue upsetting you since they will hurt!

5. ALWAYS remain insufficiently bright, all around populated regions. With more individuals around your odds of being assaulted are immensely decreased than if you were strolling along an obscure dark road with scarcely anybody or any traffic. What's more, when you have to stroll along a mysterious dark highway, at that point I urge we carry another person with you, and you need a solid ground-breaking walk and demonstrate that you look sure. If somebody looks sure and solid, they are more averse to be assaulted. Additionally, I advise purchasing pepper splash to keep in your sack or pocket consistently. Also, for your vehicle you ought to have something, for example, a bat just if you get hopped by more than one individual because there is scarcely anyone who could take on at least five folks exposed gave and win.

Defending Yourself in a Fight

If you don't have the foggiest idea how to shield yourself in a battle, you would one be able today end up in genuine threat.

Not at all like what we see on TV or in the motion pictures, most genuine rough clashes:

1. Are Over In Less Than 10 Seconds;

2. Happen Rapidly and Unexpectedly;

3. Include Weapons as well as Surprisingly Vicious Tactics; and

4. End With One Party Seriously Injured

With no viable self-defense preparing, you could without much of a stretch end up on the losing end of a vicious battle - not somewhere that you ever need to be.

As a self-defense instructor and veteran of various savage clashes, I realize that a bit of preparing can go far. It could mean the contrast between leaving safe or leaving the scene in an emergency vehicle.

Top Tips For Defending Yourself In A Fight

STRIKE FIRST: If somebody shows, through their activities, that they have a goal to hurt you physically, don't sit tight for them to make that first move. When you foresee an immediate risk of peril, strike before it is past the point of no return.

TARGET THE VITAL AREAS: Strike at the most powerless focuses on the adversary's body. These are areas that can't be molded (toughened up, for example, the eyes, throat, sun oriented plexus, crotch, and knees. Assaulting any of these fundamental areas adequately will bring about quick torment as well as damage to your adversary, allowing you to catch up with different systems - or escape.

FOLLOW THROUGH AGGRESSIVELY: Unless you flee, DO NOT ease up after your underlying strike. The ideal approach to shield yourself is to be the assailant. Catch up with a blast of attacks. If you are able and sure with taking downs and holds, utilize them. Regardless, don't stop until you are 100% certain that the danger is killed.

A certified self-defense instructor can help you in building up the aptitudes and certainty that you have to guard yourself against any assailant and end a rough clash rapidly.

Try not to go one more day without realizing how to guard yourself in a battle.

Road Fighting Techniques - How to Defend Yourself Easily!

If you need to have the option to shield yourself, you can gain proficiency with the methods of urban self-defense to remain secure.

Regardless of the way that they're talented in the preparation they've experienced, many dark belts that run combative techniques, schools don't generally have any involvement in road battling and self-defense. Those of you who attempt to take classes at the YMCA or the exercise center trying to get some answers concerning road battling will only be hitting the sack in tedious developments.

Every one of these classes shows you how to do is perform moves that may seem surprising, yet when you genuinely need to battle somebody, they will be futile; you should augment your preparation and strive to use these viable moves. You'll need to get the best possible hardware, such as competing gloves, a cup, better than average rec center shoes, a hand to hand fighting protective cap, and such to prepare for road battling. Legitimate, customary preparing consistently will give you the best probability that, if you get into a battle, you'll leave away as the victor.

You need to practice your brain just as your body. Getting amazed and found napping will be similarly as savage as not being physically arranged for a battle, so buckle down. Ensure you are knowledgeable about the genuine struggle so you can bargain and make do with the burdens battle includes. Keeping your quiet as opposed to being loaded up with dread will build your chances of winning. Come to the heart of the matter where you won't get diverted when hit in the appendages. When you have a touch of involvement added to your repertoire, begin not utilizing defensive rigging as you fight, enabling you to know your body notwithstanding a battle. Preparing your body to become acclimated with the impacts of a fight will help you more than anything on this occasion.

You genuinely need to exploit books, classes, and recordings that instruct legitimate road battling systems. If you would prefer not to transform into only one more dead body in the city, you must probably prepare your body adequately. With actual fighting, you'll genuinely be trying the breaking points of your substantial potential.

When you get assaulted, genuine competing will prepare you to have the option to anticipate each blow, be quiet in the circumstance, and enable you to endure a shot such that will keep you in the battle. You need to consistently prepare with the dynamic struggle to make your body and psyche. When you need to know how to road battle, you need to do fighting continuously.

Make sure to set objectives for yourself and train as hard and as frequently as possible. You can prepare yourself to gain proficiency with the impulses of battle as you wear your defensive hardware. Locate a perfect, calm spot to make your battling aptitudes in harmony. If you keep it correct when you figure out how to battle, you'll be better prepared to deal with yourself in a genuine battle circumstance.

Defending Yourself From Getting Raped

Assault. This single word speaks to one of the terrifying encounters a lady will ever confront. In spite of the awfulness, the word summons it is significant for a lady to realize that there are steps they can take to enable themselves to forestall a sexual assault. The motivation behind this part is to give lady approaches to avoid rape, and give women devices to protect themselves should they ever be assaulted by an aggressor.

Like some other wrongdoing assault is frequently wrongdoing of chance. It is in this manner significant that a lady knows about her surroundings consistently. When strolling in parking areas or carports, walk unquestionably and at an energetic pace. Be cautious when individuals stop to approach headings or to request cash. Continuously answer from separation and never get excessively near somebody who is addressing you from a vehicle. Be additional mindful you are in a domain where liquor is being served. When you are in a club or bar, never leave your beverage unattended. If for reasons unknown you do go, request a new drink when you return. Never acknowledge a drink from somebody you don't have the foggiest idea. Above all, trust your impulses. Numerous women allow themselves to be set in perilous circumstance because of a paranoid fear of being discourteous or seeming suspicious. If time gives you a pure inclination, there is most likely a reason. Tune in to that feeling and act appropriately.

In spite of your earnest attempts at evading peril, you may wind up in a circumstance where you are eye to eye with an attacker and assault appears to be up and coming. In cases like this, it is imperative to stay calm and confident. Attackers assault because they ache for power and looking to fulfill that requirement for power by mortifying and controlling another person. Crying and asking will give the result he is searching for, and these practices will probably urge him to do the assault. Try to attract thoughtfulness regarding yourself by hollering fire. Fire is a superior decision than "Help" or "Assault" since encompassing individuals may waver to engage with legitimate issues or a conceivable hazardous circumstance. Shouting "fire" will draw the consideration of spectators making the consideration be attracted to you and the attacker. A particular caution can be viable in both attracting thoughtfulness regarding yourself just as making physical torment the attacker's ears. If nobody is around trying serenely talking, slowing down for a time, or tell the aggressor, you have an STD.

At the point when physically shielding yourself against a male culprit, the main safeguard move that strikes a chord is to either kick or knee the man in the crotch. This isn't a fitting resistance move. It is simple for a man to see this move coming, and he is generally on a gatekeeper for it. It is barely noticeable this territory, and a bombed endeavor will annoy the man further. Stepping hard on the highest point of the foot or kicking the shins or the knee top is similarly as powerful and a lot simpler to execute effectively. Spots like the YMCA and neighborhood law enforcement organizations can regularly give data on self-preservation classes that can enable you to learn other physical self-protection moves.

There are numerous gadgets available that give no deadly types of self-protection. Pepper sprays can weaken a criminal without causing changeless physical harm. They are lightweight simple to utilize and can be used from a good ways from the culprit when picking a protection shower search for one that contains an OC detailing. Not at all like different sorts of pepper sprays, items with OC formulations cause physical responses inside the body and will be successful on all individuals including the individuals who are drunk or in a perspective that makes them careless in regards to physical agony.

Stun firearms are another non deadly yet exceedingly powerful self-preservation choice. Like OC pepper sprays, stun weapons accomplish something beyond cause physical torment. They cause disturbances in the skeletal, sensory system that will cripple a potential attacker for as long as 45 minutes. One inconvenience of stun weapons is that they do necessitate that an individual makes physically contacts the assailant with the stun firearm. It is along these lines imperative to consider the size and length of the stun weapon. It is a smart thought to physically stun the aggressor first by utilizing the resistance move referenced before in this article, for example, kicking the shins or stepping the foot.

When you are in a circumstance when you are in peril of an assault, you reserve the privilege to utilize anything available to you to ensure yourself. The conceivable weapon can be your vehicle keys a handle of a brush or items in your shopping sack. Regurgitating on you assailant could likewise repulse him. While you reserve the privilege to shield yourself, be careful in utilizing whatever can be viewed as a hostile weapon, for example, a firearm or blade. State laws shift broadly on the agreeableness of the utilization of these weapons. Regardless of whether no charges get squeezed against you for utilizing these weapons in self-preservation, you may wind up being sued by your assailant for harming him while he was trying to assault you!

The world can be a terrifying and hazardous spot. Learning how to deal with these circumstances can empower us to remain safe despite the threat.

Defending Yourself - In All Matters

Ladies are as yet attempting to locate their exact spot that relates to the worth they add to the general public. As moms, they sustain the youthful. As spouses, they adjust. As sisters, they counsel. As girls, they watch out for their older folks.

A noteworthy reason for stress for a lady nowadays is assaulted by others. They have to protect themselves against these assaults. Presently attacks need not be just physical. First ladies ought to comprehend the kinds of attacks they face both at home, in the public arena, and at work. Here are the most basic ones and a few hints on the most proficient method to protect yourself.

PHYSICAL - These can be by a mugger, an abuser, a violator or (in all honesty) from over-brutal kids. It can emerge from complete outsiders to individuals who are near you.

Tips: learn self-protection. Maintain a strategic distance from spots you can be defenseless -, for example, obscured parking garages or stairs, late-night lifts and unusual pieces of a town. Likewise, learn "gaze intently at" strategy. Assault from a grown-up ought to be countered first by not demonstrating any dread because an assailant is extremely a weakling and a harasser on a fundamental level. The minute you show you are not apprehensive and are fit for protecting yourself, you have won a large portion of the fight. Utilize realistically. When the individual is intoxicated and waving a firearm, walk or flee, or call for assistance. Assault by kids ought to never be endured even though guardians may downplay it. Kids who discover excitement in hitting or scratching will turn progressively rough. So once more, gaze intently at and immovably state no. Next time the tyke attempts to kick, immovably get hold of his arm and land NO! Regardless of whether it is another person's youngster. It is never a smart thought to whine to the parent first - manage it yourself, at that point, gripe. That way, the tyke will discover that you are not to be played with.

MENTAL - this may happen in the workplace when your manager or associate is attempting to be a twitch or practice mental torment on you. It can likewise be from your mate or relatives.

Tips: don't give the tormentor a chance to push your catches. The most noticeably awful thing you can do is lose self-assurance due to what is said- - that is absolutely what the tormentors need from you, and afterward, they have you where they need you. Solidly, serenely express your position. If the other party participates in yelling or shouting, let them completion and after that state, "I figure you should quiet down and carry on like a grown-up proficient I realize you can be. Give us a chance to visit when you are thinking and talking reasonably, will we?" After two seconds, leave. Likewise, search for an example of badgering and don't be hesitant to propose advising, or on account of the office, go to Human Resources or the following level director. Under the law, a chief can't disregard objections and needs to make a move.

Monetary - this can be through tricks or relatives or companions "mooching."

Tips: never work together exclusively on trust. This incorporates contributing cash (recall what occurred the kindred who duped companions who helped with him and brought them down for billions? These companions indiscriminately confided in him and never addressed things that were not typical in speculation the executives. So, get your work done. It merits the additional cash to pay a bookkeeper, a legal counselor, or even a legal bookkeeper to look at the plan for authenticity and foundation.

The most effective method to Defend Yourself With a Stun Gun

If you are ever stood up to by an aggressor while strolling, running, or getting in or out of your vehicle, you can effectively protect yourself with a stun weapon. A stun firearm is a little electrical gadget with two short terminals reaching out from its surface. It is small enough to fit into the palm of your hand. Whenever activated, it produces a high voltage; however, practically no amperage. This is the reason it is non-deadly and unfit to shock anybody. The amperage is the thing that causes severe damage, not the voltage.

A stun weapon will in a split second immobilize an attacker with a three to five-second touch. The high voltage immediately converts blood sugar into lactic corrosive. This right away drains the attacker's muscle vitality, and the assailant is left without the capacity to move. Simultaneously, the neurological driving forces which coordinate, and controls muscle development is intruded. The attacker further loses balance, moves toward becoming befuddle and can never again stand. This condition will last from five to ten minutes. You ought to have all that could be needed time to get to a protected area.

Stun weapons are increasingly viable when an attacker is contacted over the waste line to the upper shoulders. The whole body will be influenced. If only an arm or leg is reached, you risk merely affecting that piece of the body. At different occasions, a potential assault might be hindered by merely releasing the stun weapon in mid-air. The cathodes produce a loud scaring popping sound.

It doesn't make a difference how huge an assailant is or whether the attacker is affected by liquor or opiates; it will be successful. It makes an emotional, chemical response and meddles with the aggressor's neurological framework. This is something outside the ability to control an aggressor. Will and quality are superfluous. A model would put an elephant under sedation. Regardless of how enormous or powerful an elephant is, a little sedative spot can cut it down.

It is likewise viable and will effectively go through garments. For whatever length of time that the battery is charged, it very well may be terminated on various occasions at numerous attackers. If external contact you, there will be no electric stun or chargeback to you. The amperage is too low to even think about creating a voyaging circuit. The voltage remains between the terminals and to the assailant. The higher the voltage rating of a stun weapon, the quicker it will debilitate the objective.

Conclusion

If you have once found yourself among the group of people who often wonder why humans act the way they do, it is a great pleasure to have had this rollercoaster ride with you around everything you need to know about dark psychology and mind control, how it works and why people use it.

At the beginning of life, psychologists say humans are born in a state known as "tabula rasa," which in English translates to a "blank slate." Therefore, it is the interaction of nature and nurture of people that forms the personality of every human. Some may be smarter than others, while some will not be as smart.

Interestingly, the smart ones are the ones that can easily make use of mind control techniques to make their way through any situation. On the surface, these people may seem to just be going about life like every other human, but beyond the surface there are a lot of things going on within their psyche. They are always on the lookout for gestures, perceptions and even intuitions. These are the factors that will determine the way they relate to the things and the people around them.

With the use of mind control techniques, people can manipulate other people and situations so that they will be able to get the things they want whenever they want them. With the techniques discussed in this book, you have discovered ways to make sure that everything works in your favor. You can either brainwash, manipulate, seduce or even hypnotize your target(s) to get your desired result.

Those that are not as smart will always fall prey to this kind of mind control techniques. They will always be at the receiving end of situations involving dark psychology. Mind controllers, instead of seeing people as partners with whom they can work with to achieve great results, would rather see others as tools to be used. This will result in adverse psychological effects that could get as serious as losing one's mind and sense of self. What's more, gaining control of the mind of another person can lead them to depression and suicide if it is not well managed.

In closing, this book has given you all you need to know about mind control. It is hoped by at this point you have learned how to spot, avoid and use these tools. Remember, mind control is not only about negativity, it can also be put to some positive use. Whatever you choose to use it for, this book has surely brought you all you need to make use of it.

Good luck!